G.E. Syme T.W. Ireland

PRENTICE-HALL ACCOUNTING

Student Workbook

A

(Chapters 1 – 12
and Summary Exercise)

Prentice-Hall Canada Inc.

Canadian Cataloguing in Publication Data

Syme, G. E.
Prentice-Hall accounting. Student workbook A (chapters 1–12)

Supplement to: Syme, G. E. Prentice-Hall accounting. Ch. 1–12.
ISBN 0-13-715731-0

1. Accounting — Problems, exercises, etc.
I. Ireland, T. W. II. Title.

HF5635.S922 1990 657'.042 C89-090695-5

Also available:
Student Text 0-13-715939-0
Teacher's Guide 0-13-715756-8 (includes Computer Files disks)
Supplementary Material: Teacher's Key A (Chapters 1–12) 0-13-715715-0
Teacher's Key B (Chapters 13–18) 0-13-715723-1
Student Workbook B (Chapters 13–18) 0-13-715749-5

PRENTICE-HALL INC., Englewood Cliffs, New Jersey
PRENTICE-HALL INTERNATIONAL, INC., London
PRENTICE-HALL OF AUSTRALIA, PTY., LTD., Sydney
PRENTICE-HALL OF INDIA, PVT., LTD., New Delhi
PRENTICE-HALL OF JAPAN, INC., Tokyo
PRENTICE-HALL OF SOUTHEAST ASIA (PTE.), LTD., Singapore
EDITORA PRENTICE-HALL DO BRASIL, LTDA., Rio de Janeiro
PRENTICE-HALL HISPANOAMERICANA, S.A., Mexico

ISBN 0-13-715731-0

Project Editors: Julia Lee, Denyse O'Leary
Production Editor: Pam Young
Production Co-ordinator: Crystale Chalmers
Typesetting: LaserVision Graphics Ltd.

10 11 12 DPC 09 08 07

Printed and bound in Canada

Contents

Preface

Prentice-Hall Accounting Student Workbooks A and *B* supply all the business papers and accounting forms required to complete the exercises in the student text. *Teacher's Key A (Chapters 1–12)* and *B (Chapters 13–18)* are an exact replica of the Workbooks, with the answers to all textbook and Workbook questions and exercises keyed in.

Many teachers find it useful to be able to show the correct answers to their students. For this reason, we are giving users of the *Prentice-Hall Accounting* text permission to reproduce any or all of the pages in the Teacher's Keys. You may wish to make overheads, handouts, or displays for your bulletin board. However you wish to do it, we hope you will use this material to the full.

Teacher's Keys A and B supplement the Workbooks. These manuals are designed to assist teachers by supplying worked-out solutions for all exercises, answers for all review questions, and comments on the case studies. *Teacher's Key A* answers questions in Chapters 1 through 12 and the Summary Exercise; *Teacher's Key B* answers questions in Chapters 13 through 18, including the Supplementary Exercise. Computer exercises requiring actual programming are not dealt with in the *Teacher's Keys*, but in the *Prentice-Hall Accounting* Computer Files and in the *Teacher's Guide.*

Finally, a *Teacher's Guide* is available for the program. For each chapter of the student text, this guide offers:

- an overview of the chapter;
- a chapter schedule, indicating the approximate time each section should take to teach;
- comments for each section within the chapter, including suggestions for the introduction of a topic, ideas on how to extend a particular concept, and comments on section exercises, as well as notes about extra materials required (e.g., black-line masters, an overhead projector, supplementary books);
- comments on end-of-chapter exercises;
- comments on the careers and entrepreneur opportunities;
- black-line masters to illustrate the major concepts covered in the chapter;
- two tests, including comprehension questions as well as exercises. Selected chapters also have computer knowledge quizzes. (There are no tests for Chapter 1.)
- an appendix on teaching about computers in accounting;
- disks containing the masters for the hands-on computer exercises.

G.E.S. T.W.I.

Chapter 1 Accounting and Business

ANSWERS TO CHAPTER 1 REVIEW QUESTIONS (text, p. 11)

1. ______
2. ______
3. ______
4. ______
5. ______
6. ______
7. ______
8. ______
9. ______
10. ______
11. ______
12. ______
13. ______
14. ______
15. ______
16. ______
17. ______
18. ______
19. ______
20. ______
21. ______

 Name________________ Date____________

ANSWERS TO CHAPTER 1 REVIEW QUESTIONS (cont.)

22. ________________________________

23. ________________________________

 Name________________ Date________________

ANSWERS TO CHAPTER 1 EXERCISES (text, p. 12)

USING YOUR KNOWLEDGE

1. ____________
2. ____________
3. ____________
4. ____________
5. ____________
6. ____________
7. ____________
8. ____________
9. ____________
10. ____________
11. ____________
12. ____________
13. ____________
14. ____________
15. ____________

 Name________________ Date________________

ANSWERS TO CHAPTER 1 EXERCISES (cont.)

Exercise 2, p. 12

1. The work of a(n) ________________ is clerical in nature.
2. The work of a(n) ________________ is concerned with routine matters.
3. The term ________ is gradually being replaced with the term ________ clerk.
4. A(n) ________________ ensures that the supporting documents are present and correct for every transaction.
5. A(n) ________ ensures that generally acceptable accounting principles are followed.
6. A(n) ________________ records the accounting entries in the books of account.
7. A(n) ________________ makes the payroll calculations.
8. A(n) ________ prepares reports based on the data produced on the accounting system.
9. A(n) ________________ carries out all the necessary banking transactions.
10. A(n) ________ participates in management meetings.
11. A qualified ________ has a high-level position.
12. For centuries, all ________ was handwritten.
13. Many small businesses still do their ________ by hand.

ANSWERS TO CHAPTER 1 EXERCISES (cont.)

Exercise 3, p. 13

1. Which of the following does not fit?
   a. An accounting clerk verifies source documents.
   b. An accounting clerk ensures that the ledger balances.
   c. An accounting clerk works neatly to guard against errors.
   d. An accounting clerk studies tax bulletins to keep up to date.

2. Which of the following does not fit?
   a. An accounting clerk works out accounting entries.
   b. An accounting clerk, together with the owner, compares this year's and last year's income statements.
   c. An accounting clerk records accounting entries in the books.
   d. An accounting clerk inquires about a suspected error made by the bank.

3. Which of the following does not fit?
   a. An accountant is a professional person.
   b. An accountant has a broad knowledge of "accounting."
   c. An accountant ensures the accuracy of the payroll deductions.
   d. An accountant discusses the business's "cash flow" with the owners.

4. Which of the following does not fit?
   a. An accountant talks about the final qualifying exams.
   b. An accountant investigates the credit rating of a new customer.
   c. An accountant is promoted to vice-president.
   d. An accountant is ill; a meeting with the bank manager has to be cancelled.

5. Which of the following does not fit?
   a. The computer is an ideal machine for use in an accounting environment.
   b. The computer can handle large quantities of data.
   c. The computer produces better profit figures.
   d. The computer can provide information for management very quickly.

Name_______________ Date_______________

CAREER David Green/Student in Accounts

ANSWERS TO DISCUSSION QUESTIONS (text, p. 15)

1.

2.

3.

4.

5.

6.

Chapter 2 The Balance Sheet

ANSWERS TO SECTION 2.1 REVIEW QUESTIONS (text, p.18)

Financial Position

1. ____
   ____
   ____
2. ____
3. ____
4. ____
5. ____
6. ____
7. ____
8. ____
9. ____
10. ____
11. ____

ANSWERS TO SECTION 2.1 EXERCISES (text, p.19)

Exercise 1, p. 19

1. ________________ 5. ________________
2. ________________ 6. ________________
3. ________________ 7. ________________
4. ________________ 8. ________________

Exercise 2, p. 19

1. ________________
2. ________________
3. ________________

Exercise 3, p. 19

Office furniture ________________
An amount owed to H. Krueger, a creditor ________________
Land ________________

ANSWERS TO SECTION 2.1 EXERCISES (cont.)

Ex. 3 (cont.)

Supplies ____________
Bank loan ____________
Buildings ____________
An unpaid heating bill ____________
An amount owed by R. Jonas, a debtor ____________
Mortgage payable ____________
Trucks ____________
A Canada Savings Bond ____________
An account receivable ____________
An account payable ____________

Exercise 4, p. 19

$37 486.49	–	$11 547.80	=	________
A	–	L	=	OE

Exercise 5, p. 19

	Assets	Liabilities
	$150 000	$70 000
	+ 70 000	–20 000
19 – 2		

Owner's Equity ________ – ________ = ________

Exercise 6, p. 19

____

Exercise 7, p. 19

____

Exercise 8, p. 19

____

Exercise 9, p. 19

1. *ASSETS*

Name ______________________ Date ________________

ANSWERS TO SECTION 2.1 EXERCISES (cont.)

Ex. 9 (cont.)

2. LIABILITIES

3. EQUITY: ______________________

Exercise 10, p. 20

ASSETS

LIABILITIES

NET WORTH: ______________________

Chapter 2

Name________________________ Date________________

ANSWERS TO SECTION 2.2 REVIEW QUESTIONS (text, p. 26)

The Balance Sheet

1. ____________________
2. ____________________
3. ____________________
4. ____________________
5. ____________________
6. ____________________
7. ____________________
8. ____________________
9. ____________________
10. ____________________
11. ____________________
12. ____________________
13. ____________________
14. ____________________

 Name____________________ Date_______________

ANSWERS TO SECTION 2.2 EXERCISES (text, p. 26)

Exercise 1, p. 26

Exercise 2, p. 27

ANSWERS TO SECTION 2.2 EXERCISES (cont.)

Exercise 3, p. 27

Exercise 4, p. 28 (Workbook Exercise)

There are seven errors in the following balance sheet presentation. Find the errors and make a list of them.

BALANCE SHEET
MUSIC MAKERS
AUG. 31, 19 —

Assets		*Liabilities*	
Accounts Receivable		Bank Loan	$ 3 500.00
W. Strothers	$ 128.40	Accounts Payable	
Waller Company	160.50	Circle of Sound	270.00
Supplies	74.50	A to Z Recordings	120.00
Sound Equipment	9 467.00		$ 3 500.00
Tapes and Records	2 674.00	*Mary Menari*	
Truck	7 500.00	Equity	17 269.40
Bank Balance	765.00		$20 769.40
	$20 769.40		

ANSWERS TO SECTION 2.2 EXERCISES (cont.)

Exercise 4 (cont.)

1.
2.
3.
4.
5.
6.
7.

ANSWERS TO SECTION 2.3 REVIEW QUESTIONS (text, p. 29)

Claims against the Assets

1.
2.
3.
4.
5.

ANSWERS TO SECTION 2.3 EXERCISES (text, p. 29)

Exercise 1, p. 29

ANSWERS TO SECTION 2.3 EXERCISES (cont.)

Ex. 1 (cont.)

Exercise 2, p. 30

1.

Carla's Interior Design

Balance Sheet

July 31, 19 —

2.

Chapter 2

Name ______________________ Date ______________

ANSWERS TO SECTION 2.4 REVIEW QUESTIONS (text, p. 32)

Generally Accepted Accounting Principles

1. ______________________________

2. ______________________________

3. ______________________________

4. ______________________________

5. ______________________________

6. ______________________________

7. ______________________________

ANSWERS TO SECTION 2.4 EXERCISES (text, p. 32)

Exercise 1, p. 32

ASSETS	**AMOUNT**	**BUSINESS**	**PERSONAL**
Accounts Receivable	$ 27 460		
Boat and Motor	16 520		
Business Bank Balance	1 852		
Business Automobiles	48 054		
Furniture and Appliances	6 528		
Government Bonds of Owner	20 000		
House and Lot	99 600		
Office Furniture and Equipment	18 324		
Office Supplies	3 545		
Owner's Automobiles	18 657		
Paving Materials	55 326		
Personal Bank Balance	1 258		
Plant Property and Buildings	125 358		
Summer Cottage	65 874		
Trucks and Equipment	285 657		
Total Assets			
LIABILITIES			
Accounts Payable	3 500		
Business Bank Loan	56 000		
Mortgage on Plant Property	75 000		
Mortgage on House and Lot	60 000		
Mortgage on Summer Cottage	22 300		
Owed to Finance Co. — Co. Equipment	136 522		
Total Liabilities			
OWNER'S EQUITY			

 Name ______________ Date ______________

ANSWERS TO SECTION 2.4 EXERCISES (cont.)

Exercise 2, p. 34

1. a. ______________
   b. ______________

2. a. ______________
   b. ______________

3. a. ______________
   b. ______________

4. a. ______________
   b. ______________

5. a. ______________
   b. ______________

6. a. ______________
   b. ______________

ANSWERS TO COMPUTER REVIEW 2.5 QUESTIONS (text, p. 37)

The Accounting Spreadsheet

1. ______________
2. ______________
3. ______________
4. ______________
5. ______________
6. ______________
7. ______________
8. ______________
9. ______________

ANSWERS TO COMPUTER REVIEW 2.5 QUESTIONS (cont.)

10. ______________________________

11. ______________________________

12. ______________________________

13. ______________________________

Chapter 2

Name____________________________ Date__________________

ANSWERS TO CHAPTER 2 EXERCISES (text, p. 39)

USING YOUR KNOWLEDGE

Exercise 1, p. 39

For each of the following questions, write the letter that represents the best possible answer.

1. The financial position of a business is ____
   a. the difference between total assets and total liabilities.
   b. represented by all of the assets, liabilities, and the capital.
   c. the same as the "net worth" of the business.

2. If the total assets increase by $10 000 and the total liabilities decrease by $10 000, the capital will ____
   a. increase by $20 000.
   b. be unchanged.
   c. decrease by $20 000.

3. Which one of the following is not true? ____
   a. A – C = L.
   b. A – L = C.
   c. A + L = C.
   d. A = L + C.

4. A balance sheet shows ____
   a. all of the owner's assets and liabilities.
   b. a financial picture of the business on a certain date.
   c. the progress of the business over a period of time.

5. Which one of the following is not true? ____
   a. The heading of a balance sheet shows the date as of which it was prepared.
   b. Assets are listed in the order of their liquidity.
   c. Accounts receivable are considered to be a liquid asset.
   d. Personal assets have no place on the business balance sheet.
   e. A truck which cost $10 000 and on which $6 000 is owed is listed on the balance sheet at $4 000.

6. Abbreviations may be used on financial statements ____
   a. when it is necessary to crowd things to conserve space.
   b. to save time in preparing the statements.
   c. in a company name if the abbreviation is a formal part of the name.

7. Which one of the following is not true? ____
   Columnar paper helps the accountant
   a. to add columns more accurately.
   b. to make records easier to read.
   c. to make the records more attractive.
   d. to make recordkeeping go more quickly.

8. Which one of the following is not true? ____
   a. Ruled lines are used to underline headings.

ANSWERS TO CHAPTER 2 EXERCISES (cont.)

Exercise 1 (cont.)

b. Ruled lines are used to indicate that columns of numbers are to be totaled.
c. Ruled lines are necessary to separate sections of the balance sheet.
d. Ruled lines are doubled to indicate a final total.

9. Before a business is closed down, the equation for it is:
   Assets (125 000) = Liabilities (37 000) + Equity (88 000).
   If assets of $70 000 are sold for $20 000, assets of 50 000 are sold for $90 000, and the remaining assets stay the same, the equation will become ____
   a. $ 55 000 = $ 37 000 + $ 18 000.
   b. $ 115 000 = $ 37 000 + $ 78 000.
   c. $ 75 000 = $ 37 000 + $ 38 000.
   d. $ 135 000 = $ 47 000 + $ 88 000.
   e. $ 115 000 = $ 27 000 + $ 88 000.

10. Which one of the following is not true? ____
    a. On a balance sheet short term debts are listed first.
    b. On a balance sheet there are three main totals.
    c. On a balance sheet the owner's name only appears in the heading.
    d. On a balance sheet the final totals are always on the same line.

Exercise 2, p. 40

Exercise 3, p. 41

FOR FURTHER THOUGHT

Exercise 4, p. 41

1. ____________

2. ____________

ANSWERS TO CHAPTER 2 EXERCISES (cont.)

Exercise 4 (cont.)

3. ____________________

4. ____________________

5. ____________________
6. ____________________
7. ____________________

8. ____________________

9. ____________________

10. ____________________

CASE STUDIES (text, p.42)

Case 1 *Considering the Purchase of a Business*, p. 42

1. What condition is the equipment in and is it really worth $67 600?
2. ____________________
3. ____________________
4. ____________________
5. ____________________
6. ____________________
7. ____________________
8. ____________________
9. ____________________
10. ____________________
11. ____________________

 Name ______________ Date ______________

CASE STUDIES (cont.)

Case 2 *Placing a Value on Assets*, p. 43

1. ______________________________

2. ______________________________

3. ______________________________

4. ______________________________

5.

Custom-Made Products

Balance Sheet

6. ______________________________

 Name__________ Date__________

ENTREPRENEUR Samuel Essex/Sole Proprietor

ANSWERS TO DISCUSSION QUESTIONS (text, p. 46)

1.

2.

3.

4.

5.

6.

7.

 Name____________________________ Date ____________________

Chapter 3 Analyzing Changes in Financial Position

ANSWERS TO SECTION 3.1 REVIEW QUESTIONS (text, p. 47)

Business Transactions

1. ____
2. ____
3. ____
4. ____

ANSWERS TO SECTION 3.1 EXERCISES (text, p. 48)

Exercise 1, p. 48

1. ____________________
2. ____________________
3. ____________________
4. ____________________
5. ____________________
6. ____________________
7. ____________________
8. ____________________

Exercise 2, p. 48

Given that a transaction is a financial event that requires changing the statement of financial position, decide whether or not each of the following is a transaction. You are working for Ace Collection Agency of Regina, Saskatchewan, owned by Ingrid Lencz.

1. $40 cash was paid for gasoline for the company automobile.
2. Ingrid Lencz paid $15 out of her own pocket for lunch.
3. Ingrid's personal car was damaged and needed a $500 repair job.
4. A $250 service was performed for a customer who paid cash.
5. A leased typewriter broke down and needed to be replaced at no cost to the businss. The man who came with the replacement said that the new machine was a $1 500 one.
6. A customer who owed the business $1 200 makes a partial payment of $300.
7. The business bank loan was reduced by a direct payment to the bank of $1 000.
8. A burglar broke into the office and stole the leased typewriter. The business has 100 per cent replacement insurance to cover breaking and entering and theft.

ANSWERS TO SECTION 3.1 EXERCISES (cont.)

Ex. 2 (cont.)

1. ______________________ 5. ______________________
2. ______________________ 6. ______________________
3. ______________________ 7. ______________________
4. ______________________ 8. ______________________

ANSWERS TO SECTION 3.2 REVIEW QUESTIONS (text, p. 56)

Equation Analysis Sheet

1. ______________________
2. ______________________
3. ______________________
4. ______________________
5. ______________________

ANSWERS TO SECTION 3.2 EXERCISES (text, p. 56)

Exercise 1, p. 56

	ASSETS					LIABILITIES		OWNER'S EQUITY
	Cash	Account Receivable	Supplies	Office Furniture	Truck	Accounts Payable		S. Kostiuk capital
		D. Murray				Ace Supply	Pine Motors	
Opening balances	**1 000**	**50**						**1 050**

 Name______________________ Date ________________

ANSWERS TO SECTION 3.2 EXERCISES (cont.)

Exercise 2, p. 57

1., 2.

ASSETS	LIABILITIES	OWNER'S EQUITY

 Name______________________ Date ______________

ANSWERS TO SECTION 3.2 EXERCISES (cont.)

Ex. 2 (cont.)

3.

Triangle Real Estate

Balance Sheet

October 1, 19 —

ANSWERS TO SECTION 3.2 EXERCISES (cont.)

Exercise 3, p. 58

1., 2.

ASSETS							LIABILITIES		OWNER'S EQUITY

ANSWERS TO SECTION 3.2 EXERCISES (cont.)

Ex. 3 (cont.)

3. Alliance Appliance Service

Balance Sheet

October 21, 19 —

Exercise 4, p. 58 (Workbook Exercise)

Patricia Severs is a lawyer who owns her own law firm in Lethbridge, Alberta. On the morning of May 6, 19 —, the business has the following assets and liabilities:

Assets		*Liabilities*	
Cash	$ 1 761	Accounts Payable	
Accounts Receivable		Wilson's Co.	$ 356
V. Brabson	100	Beneficial Finance	10 320
T. Carlisle	50		
Office Supplies	1 442		
Office Equipment	12 330		
Automobile	17 500		

1. Set up the assets, the liabilities, and the capital on an equation analysis sheet.
2. Analyze the transactions of May 6, listed below, and record the necessary changes on the equation analysis sheet.

ANSWERS TO SECTION 3.2 EXERCISES (cont.)

Ex. 4 (cont.)

3. After completing transaction 5, calculate the new balances, and ensure that the equation is still in balance. Then prepare a new balance sheet.

Transactions of May 6

1. $1 750 cash is paid for an air conditioner for the office.
2. Because the cash position of the business is very low, Pat Severs transfers $4 000 cash from her personal bank account into the business.
3. A cash payment of $815 is paid to Beneficial Finance.
4. Arthur Kushner, a client of Pat Severs, is given legal advice for which he is charged $200. Mr. Kushner pays immediately.
5. Pat Severs has a minor repair done to her automobile. The bill of $110 is paid immediately.

ANSWERS TO SECTION 3.2 EXERCISES (cont.)

Ex. 4 (cont.)

1., 2.

ASSETS	LIABILITIES	OWNER'S EQUITY

ANSWERS TO SECTION 3.2 EXERCISES (cont.)

Ex. 4 (cont.)

3.

Patricia Severs

Balance Sheet

May 6, 19—

ANSWERS TO SECTION 3.3 REVIEW QUESTIONS (text, p. 59)

Summary of Steps in Analyzing a Transaction

1. ____________________

2. ____________________

3. ____________________

4. ____________________

5. ____________________

 Name ____________ Date ____________

ANSWERS TO SECTION 3.4 REVIEW QUESTIONS (text, p. 61)

Introduction to Source Documents

1. ____________
2. ____________
3. ____________
4. ____________
5. ____________
6. ____________
7. ____________

ANSWERS TO SECTION 3.4 EXERCISES (text, p. 61)

Exercise 1, p. 61

1. ____________
2. ____________
3. ____________
4. ____________
5. ____________
6. ____________
7. ____________

Exercise 2, p. 62

1. ____________
2. ____________
3. ____________
4. ____________
5. ____________
6. ____________
7. ____________
8. ____________
9. ____________

 Name ________ Date ________

ANSWERS TO SECTION 3.4 EXERCISES (cont.)

Exercise 3, p. 63

1. ________
2. ________
3. ________
4. ________
5. ________

Exercise 4, p. 63

1. ________
2. ________

ANSWERS TO COMPUTER REVIEW 3.5 QUESTIONS (text, p. 66)

1. ________
2. ________
3. ________
4. ________
5. ________

COMMUNICATE IT (text, p. 66)

____

Chapter 3

Name________________________ Date __________________

ANSWERS TO CHAPTER 3 EXERCISES (text, p. 67)

USING YOUR KNOWLEDGE

Exercise 1, p. 67

1. ____
2. ____
3. ____
4. ____
5. ____

Exercise 2, p. 68

1. ____
2. ____
3. ____
4. ____
5. ____

Exercise 3, p. 68

Year	Assets	Liabilities	Equity
19 -1	$ 85 000	1.	$60 000
19-2	$115 000	2.	3.

Exercise 4, p. 68

Exercise 5, p. 68

 Name______________________ Date ______________

ANSWERS TO CHAPTER 3 EXERCISES (cont.)

Exercise 6, p. 68 (Workbook Exercise)

Complete the following schedule for the business of Lara Segal, a land surveyor in Fredericton, New Brunswick. For each transaction indicate the change in the Total Assets, the Total Liabilities, or the Equity by placing a plus sign, a minus sign, or a zero, together with the amount in the appropriate space in the first three columns. Indicate no change by placing a checkmark in column 4.

TRANSACTIONS	TOTAL ASSETS	TOTAL LIABILITIES	OWNER'S EQUITY	NO CHANGE
1. Purchased $200 of supplies but did not pay for them.	+200	+200		
2. Purchased $100 of supplies; paid cash.				
3. Paid off a creditor with $50 cash.				
4. Purchased $100 of supplies; paid $20 cash and owed the balance of $80.				
5. Received $300 cash from a debtor.				
6. Performed a $400 service for a customer who pays in cash.				
7. Performed a $210 service for a customer who has not paid yet.				
8. Discovered that $30 of supplies are spoiled; the supplies are thrown out.				
9. Sold a $200 asset for $75 cash and suffered a $125 loss.				
10. Paid a property tax bill on the due date. No previous entry had been made regarding these taxes; $250				
11. Performed a $250 service for a customer. The customer pays $50 cash and owes the balance.				
12. Purchased gasoline for the auto for cash. The gasoline is used within the day; $10.				
13. Paid the wages of an employee; $175.				
14. Received a $30 refund on car insurance.				
15. The owner takes $200 cash out of the business for her personal use.				

 Name_______________ Date _______________

ANSWERS TO CHAPTER 3 EXERCISES (cont.)

CHALLENGE EXERCISE

Exercise 7, p. 68

1., 2.

	ASSETS	LIABILITIES	OWNER'S EQUITY

 Name__________ Date __________

ANSWERS TO CHAPTER 3 EXERCISES (cont.)

Ex. 7 (cont.)

3. *Merrymen Window Washing*

Balance Sheet

November 30, 19 —

FOR FURTHER THOUGHT

Exercise 8, p. 69

1. __________
2. __________
3. __________
4. __________

 Name ______________________ Date ______________

ANSWERS TO CHAPTER 3 EXERCISES (cont.)

Ex. 8 (cont.)

5.

6.

7.

8.

9.

10.

11.

12.

Chapter 3

Name ______________________ Date ______________

CASE STUDIES (text, p. 71)

Case 1 *Is Money Better?*, p. 71

Case 2 *Can You Spend the Equity?*, p. 72

Case 3 *Checking Out a New Customer*, p. 72

1.

2.

3.

CAREER Melissa Porchuk/Student

ANSWERS TO DISCUSSION QUESTIONS (text, p. 75)

1.

2.

 Name________________ Date ________________

ANSWERS TO DISCUSSION QUESTIONS (cont.)

3. ____

4. ____

5. ____

6. ____

Chapter 4 The Simple Ledger

ANSWERS TO SECTION 4.1 REVIEW QUESTIONS (text, p. 79)

Ledger Accounts

1. ______________________________

2. ______________________________

3. ______________________________

4. ______________________________

5. ______________________________

6. ______________________________

7. ______________________________

8. ______________________________

9. ______________________________

10. ______________________________

ANSWERS TO SECTION 4.1 EXERCISES (text, p. 79)

Exercise 1, p. 79

Cash		Accounts Receivable A. Marks		Accounts Receivable C. Prentice	

ANSWERS TO SECTION 4.1 EXERCISES (cont.)

Ex. 1, (cont.)

Land

Building

Equipment

Truck

Bank Loan

Account Payable
Gem Lumber

Mortgage Payable

T. Stevens,
Capital

Exercise 2, p. 80

Cash

Account Receivable
P. Auul

Account Receivable
S. Wouke

ANSWERS TO SECTION 4.1 EXERCISES (cont.)

Ex. 2, (cont.)

Supplies	

Furniture and Equipment	

Automobile	

Account Payable A.B. Associates	

Account Payable Medico Supply	

Pauline Inaba, Capital	

Exercise 3, p. 80

Assets: ____________________

Liabilities: ____________________

A	–	L	=	OE
____	–	____	=	____

ANSWERS TO SECTION 4.2 REVIEW QUESTIONS (text, p. 88)

Debit and Credit Theory

1. ____________________
2. ____________________
   ____
3. ____________________
4. ____________________
5. ____________________
6. ____________________

 Name_______________ Date_______________

ANSWERS TO SECTION 4.2 REVIEW QUESTIONS (cont.)

7. ____________________

8. ____________________

9. ____________________

10. ____________________

11. ____________________

12. ____________________

ANSWERS TO SECTION 4.2 EXERCISES (text, p. 88)

Exercise 1, p. 88

ASSETS		=	LIABILITIES		+	OWNER'S EQUITY	
Debit	Credit		Debit	Credit		Debit	Credit

 Name________________ Date________________

ANSWERS TO SECTION 4.2 EXERCISES (cont.)

Exercise 2, p. 88

Trans-action No.	Account Names	Account Classification: Asset, Liability or Owner's Equity	Increase (+) or Decrease (–)	Debit or Credit	Amount
1	Cash	Asset	+	DR	300 –
	Account Receivable J. Parker	Asset	–	CR	300 –

 Name________________________ Date________________

ANSWERS TO SECTION 4.2 EXERCISES (cont.)

Exercise 3, p. 89 (Workbook Exercise)

Crooks Garage is a small business operated by James Crooks. Shown below are10 selected transactions of Crooks Garage. Analyze these transactions on a transaction analysis sheet. When performing your analysis, choose from the following accounts:

Cash
Accounts Receivable (various)
Supplies
Equipment
Truck
Bank Loan
Accounts Payable (various)
J. Crooks, Capital

Transactions

1. A car is repaired for a customer who pays the $450 charge in cash.
2. $170 of supplies is purchased for cash.
3. $125 is paid to Rossi Co., an account payable.
4. $90 is received from G. Rawl, an account receivable.
5. A welding unit, included in the Equipment account at $500, is run over by a truck. It is so badly damaged that it has to be thrown away.
6. A new welding unit is purchased on credit from Bly Co. at a cost of $790.
7. For the repair of his car, F. Stefryk pays $100 cash and owes $250, the balance of the repair charge.
8. Arrangements are made with the bank to borrow $6 000. A promissory note for this amount is signed by Mr. Crooks for the bank, after which the bank provides the business with $6 000 cash.
9. Albert McCann, a mechanic employed by Crooks Garage, is paid wages of $375.
10. A towing service is performed for a customer for $40 cash.

 Name ____________________ Date ________________

ANSWERS TO SECTION 4.2 EXERCISES (cont.)

Ex. 3 (cont.)

Transaction No.	Account Names	Account Classification: Asset, Liability or Owner's Equity	Increase (+) or Decrease (–)	Debit or Credit	Amount

ANSWERS TO SECTION 4.2 EXERCISES (cont.)

Exercise 4, p. 89 (Workbook Exercise)

Reliable Janitorial Service is owned and operated by Margot Finley. The ledger for the business has the following accounts. The numbers to the left are for this exercise only.

Number	Account
1	Cash
2	Account Receivable — M. King
3	Supplies
4	Equipment
5	Truck
6	Account Payable — Special Chemicals
7	Bank Loan
8	M. Finley, Capital

Given below are a series of transactions in a chart. For each transaction, give the accounting entry by placing correctly the account numbers in the columns provided.

Transaction 1 is completed for you.

	Transaction	Debit	Credit
1.	Purchased cleaning supplies from Special Chemicals Co. but did not pay for them.	3	6
2.	Purchased equipment for cash.		
3.	Performed a cleaning service for a customer who paid cash.		
4.	Performed a cleaning service for M. King who agreed to pay in 30 days.		
5.	Received the amount owed by M. King.		
6.	Paid the amount owed to Special Chemicals.		
7.	Borrowed money from the bank.		
8.	The owner took money out of the business for her personal use.		
9.	Supplies were spoiled and thrown out.		

ANSWERS TO SECTION 4.3 REVIEW QUESTIONS (text, p. 92)

Account Balances

1. ____

2. ____

 Name ______________________ Date ________________

ANSWERS TO SECTION 4.3 REVIEW QUESTIONS (cont.)

____

____

3. ____

____

____

4. ____

____

5. ____

____

6. ____

7. ____

____

____

____

____

8. ____

____

ANSWERS TO SECTION 4.3 EXERCISES (text, p. 92)

Exercise 1, p. 92

Cash	
250	190
1 210	48
360	512
29	

Account Receivable H. Devrie	
25	175
150	
70	
35	

Account Payable P. Helka	
30	75
45	40
	175

R. Smart, Capital	
150	3 140

1. ____

2. ____

ANSWERS TO SECTION 4.3 EXERCISES (cont.)

Exercise 2, p. 93

1. ________________________________

2. ________________________________

Exercise 3, p. 93

		Debit	Credit
1.	The left side of an account.		
2.	The balance of an account receivable.		
3.	The balance of a supplier's account.		
4.	A decrease in a liability.		
5.	An exceptional balance in the Bank account.		
6.	The balance in the equipment account.		
7.	The right side of an account.		
8.	The balance in the Bank Loan account.		
9.	An exceptional balance in an accounts payable account.		
10.	The larger side of a liability account.		
11.	A creditor's account.		
12.	A customer's account.		
13.	An increase in an asset.		
14.	A debtor's account.		

ANSWERS TO SECTION 4.4 REVIEW QUESTIONS (text, p. 97)

The Trial Balance

1. ________________________________

2. ________________________________

Name ______________________ Date ______________

ANSWERS TO SECTION 4.4 REVIEW QUESTIONS (cont.)

3. ______________________________

4. ______________________________

5. ______________________________

6. ______________________________

7. ______________________________

8. ______________________________

ANSWERS TO SECTION 4.4 EXERCISES (text, p. 98)

Exercise 1, p. 98

J. Strom

Trial Balance

December 31, 19 —

			DEBIT	CREDIT

ANSWERS TO SECTION 4.4 EXERCISES (cont.)

Exercise 2, p. 98

____

____

____

			DEBIT	CREDIT

Chapter 4 Name____________________ Date____________________

ANSWERS TO SECTION 4.4 EXERCISES (cont.)

Exercise 3, p. 99

____

____

____

			DEBIT	CREDIT

ANSWERS TO SECTION 4.4 EXERCISES (cont.)

Exercise 4, p. 99 (Workbook Exercise)

The business of Margo Anders began with a $20 000 bank deposit. After recording some transactions, her ledger appears as shown below.

Find out why the ledger does not balance.

Cash

Debit	Credit
20 000	5 000
900	10 000
500	2 000
21 400	***17 000***
(4 400)	

A/R S. Adat

Debit	Credit
500	50
500	***50***
(450)	

A/R T. Fox

Debit	Credit
1 200	
(1 200)	

Supplies

Debit	Credit
2 000	
(2 000)	

Equipment

Debit	Credit
5 000	
4 000	
(9 000)	

Trucks

Debit	Credit
25 000	
(25 000)	

Loan payable

Debit	Credit
	15 000
	(15 000)

A/P Supply House

Debit	Credit
	2 000
	4 000
	2 000
	(8 000)

M.Anders, Capital

Debit	Credit
	20 000
	500
	990
	1 200
	(22 690)

Trial Balance

DR	CR
4 400	15 000
450	8 000
1 200	22 690
2 000	
9 000	
25 000	
42 050	45 690

 Name________________ Date____________

ANSWERS TO SECTION 4.4 EXERCISES (cont.)

Ex. 4 (cont.)

1. ____________________
2. ____________________
3. ____________________

Exercise 5, p. 99 (Workbook Exercise)

Why does this ledger not balance?

Cash

4 000	9 000
10 000	250
3 000	75
375	
17 075	9 325

Acc Rec'l — P. Jarvis

3 000	3 000

Supplies

500	
75	
425	

Equipment

12 000	
9 000	
21 000	

Truck

25 000	

Bank Loan

	10 000

Acc Pay'l — Supply House

9 000	9 000
250	500
250	
(ø) 9 500	9 500

R. Howse, Capital

	41 000
	300
	735
	42 035

Trial Balance

DR	CR
7 750	10 000
425	42 035
21 000	
25 000	
54 175	52 035

1. ____________________
2. ____________________
3. ____________________

 Name________________ Date________________

ANSWERS TO CHAPTER 4 EXERCISES (text, p. 100)

USING YOUR KNOWLEDGE

Exercise 1, p. 100

Indicate whether each of the following statements is true or false by entering a "T" or an "F" in the space indicated. Explain the reason for each "F" response in the space provided.

1. A number of individual balance sheet items may appear on one account page, as long as they are shown separately. ☐
2. Many accountants use the equation analysis sheet instead of the ledger. ☐
3. There is a page in the ledger for the total assets figure. ☐
4. T–accounts are ideal for small businesses. ☐
5. The first dollar amount recorded in an account is placed on the same side as it appears on a simple balance sheet. ☐
6. There is no account for capital because it can always be found by subtracting the total assets from the total liabilities. ☐
7. A transaction analysis sheet is a permanent accounting record. ☐
8. For every transaction, there is always one debit amount and one credit amount which are equal. ☐
9. A balanced accounting entry is a correct accounting entry. ☐
10. The balance of an account that is not zero must be either a debit or a credit. ☐
11. The J.R. Dahl account in the ledger of C. Jacob is either an account payable or an account receivable. ☐
12. Eric Lai's account has a credit balance. This means that he purchased our services on credit. ☐
13. An exceptional balance merely means that it is opposite to what it would be normally. ☐
14. A customer is given a refund because of unsatisfactory service. The account of this customer would then have an exceptional balance. ☐
15. A ledger contains an exceptional balance. A trial balance cannot be taken until the exceptional item is transferred to another part of the ledger. ☐
16. A trial balance that is in balance proves that there are no errors in the accounts. ☐
17. A trial balance is taken using a printing calculator. When the total key is pressed, the figure 89.00 comes up. This is the amount of the error. ☐
18. The business buys supplies and pays cash. The accounting entry made in the accounts is Dr Cash and Cr Supplies. This causes the ledger to be out of balance. ☐
19. A correct trial balance needs to be kept only until the next one is taken. ☐

 Name________________ Date________________

ANSWERS TO CHAPTER 4 EXERCISES (cont.)

Ex. 1 (cont.)

Explanations:

ANSWERS TO CHAPTER 4 EXERCISES (cont.)

Exercise 2, p. 100 (Workbook Exercise)

1. The ledger of a small service business appears below.

ASSETS

Cash	
1 500	300
450	250
	50

Supplies	
400	

Account Receivable W. Brandt	
700	450
190	

Equipment	
3 000	
600	

LIABILITIES

Account Payable Perrier Co.	
300	500

Account Payable S. Bloom Co.	
	350

OWNER'S EQUIT

M. Barr,Capital	
50	5 1[illegible]
	1[illegible]

1. Write down the opening financial position.
2. Give a brief description of five transactions that would have caused the entries recorded in the accounts. It is not important to list these in the correct order.

 Name ______________________ Date ________________

ANSWERS TO CHAPTER 4 EXERCISES (cont.)

Ex. 2 (cont.)

2.

			DEBIT					CREDIT				

ANSWERS TO CHAPTER 4 EXERCISES (cont.)

Exercise 3, p. 100 (Workbook Exercise)

The ledger of Dorothy Prouse, a lawyer, appears below.

ASSETS

Cash

500	412
78	250
300	5 000
5 000	75

Supplies

385	
75	

Account Receivable R. Burke

125	
985	

Equipment

2 956	

Account Receivable O. Patterson

78	78

Automobile

3 050	
8 000	

LIABILITIES

Bank Loan

	5 000

Account Payable Fincham Co.

412	412

Account Payable Master Finance

	3 000

OWNER'S EQUITY

D. Prouse, Capital

250	6 682
	300
	985

1. Write down the opening financial position.
2. Describe briefly eight transactions that would have caused the entries recorded in the accounts. The order of the transactions is not important.

 Name____________________ Date_______________

ANSWERS TO CHAPTER 4 EXERCISES (cont.)

Ex. 3 (cont.)

			DEBIT	CREDIT

 Name______________________________ Date______________________

ANSWERS TO CHAPTER 4 EXERCISES (cont.)

Exercise 4, p. 101

1. ____________________
2. ____________________
3. ____________________

Exercise 5, p. 101

- ____________________
- ____________________
- ____________________

Exercise 6, p. 101

1. ____________________
2. ____________________
3. ____________________
4. ____________________

Exercise 7, p. 101

1. ____________________
2. ____________________
3. ____________________
4. ____________________
5. ____________________
6. ____________________
7. ____________________
8. ____________________
9. ____________________

Chapter 4 Name____________________ Date______________

ANSWERS TO CHAPTER 4 EXERCISES (cont.)

COMPREHENSIVE EXERCISES

Exercise 8, p. 103

1., 2.

Cash	

Account Receivable G. Anderson	

Account Receivable N. Ostrowski	

Office Supplies	

Painting Supplies	

Office Furniture	

Automobile	

Bank Loan	

Account Payable Consumers' Supply	

Account Payable Nu-Style Furniture	

Loan Payable	

A. Hoysted, Capital	

Account Receivable G. Brand	

ANSWERS TO CHAPTER 4 EXERCISES (cont.)

Ex. 8 (cont.)

3.

ANSWERS TO CHAPTER 4 EXERCISES (cont.)

Exercise 9, p. 103

Account	Debit	Credit
Cash	1 056	
Account Receivable V. Morris		
Account Receivable D. Murray	1 351	
Account Receivable A. Niemi	2 516	
Office Supplies	1 115	
Furniture and Equipment	11 916	
Properties Owned	18 042	
Automobile	27 965	
Bank Loan		19 000
Account Payable Pioneer Furniture		
Account Payable Tuck Corporation		1 520
Cathy Rogers, Capital		43 441

ANSWERS TO CHAPTER 4 EXERCISES (cont.)

Ex. 9 (cont.)

 Name________________ Date________________

ANSWERS TO CHAPTER 4 EXERCISES (cont.)

FOR FURTHER THOUGHT

Exercise 10, p. 104

1. ______
2. ______
3. ______
4. ______
5. ______
6. ______
7. ______
8. ______
9. ______
10. ______
11. ______
12. ______
13. ______
14. ______
15. ______

Chapter 4

Name ____________ Date ____________

CASE STUDIES (text, p. 105)

Case 1 *Property Value on a Balance Sheet*, p. 105

1. ____________

2. ____________

3. ____________

Case 2 *Choosing between Two Companies*, p. 106

1. ____________

2. ____________

3. ____________

ENTREPRENEUR Paul Murphy/Fab-Tech Industries

ANSWERS TO DISCUSSION QUESTIONS (text, p. 108)

1. ____________

2. ____________

3. ____________

4. ____________

 Name__________ Date__________

Chapter 5 The Expanded Ledger: Revenue, Expenses and Drawings

ANSWERS TO SECTION 5.1 REVIEW QUESTIONS (text, p. 116)

Expanding the Ledger

1. __________

2. __________

3. __________

4. __________

5. __________

6. __________

7. __________

8. __________

9. __________

10. __________

 Name______________________ Date______________

ANSWERS TO SECTION 5.1 EXERCISES (text, p. 116)

Exercise 1, p. 116

A business has the beginning financial position recorded in the schedule below. Ten simple transactions are listed in the left-hand column. Work out the revised totals for assets, liabilities, and owner's equity after each transaction. Enter these totals in your Workbook. Complete the last two columns of the chart by recording: a) the amount of change in equity (if any), and b) whether the change in equity represents revenue, expense, or drawings.

	Total Assets	Total Liabs.	Owner's Equity	Change in Equity	Revenue? Expense? Drawings?
Starting Position	10 000	6 000	4 000		
Transactions 1. Purchased $400 of supplies for future use and paid cash.					
2. Reduced bank loan by $1 000.					
3. Received $800 cash from a debtor.					
4. Sold services for $900 cash.					
5. Sold services on credit, $1 500.					
6. Paid hydro for month just ended, $125.					
7. Owner withdrew $750 cash for personal use.					
8. Paid employee's wages, $600.					
9. Purchase truck on credit, $20 000.					
10. Owner took merchandise for personal use, $250.					

Chapter 5

Name________________________ Date__________________

ANSWERS TO SECTION 5.1 EXERCISES (cont.)

Exercise 2, p. 116

DATE	DEBITS		CREDITS	
	ACCOUNT(S)	AMOUNT	ACCOUNT(S)	AMOUNT

Exercise 3, p. 118

1. The Bank account normally has a _____ balance.
2. A Revenue account normally has a _____ balance.
3. An Expense account normally has a _____ balance.
4. Paying a creditor involves a _____ entry to the creditor's account.
5. The Drawings account receives a _____ entry when the owner withdraws money for personal use.
6. A lawyer gives a refund to a customer. The Bank account will receive a _____ entry and the Revenue account will receive a _____ entry.
7. Supplies are bought on credit. The Supplies account will receive a _____ entry and the supplier's account payable will receive a _____ entry.
8. The Drawings account will not normally receive _____ entries.
9. An increase in equity can be thought of as a _____ to the Capital account.
10. Net profit can be thought of as a _____ to the Capital account.
11. Net loss can be thought of as a _____ to the Capital account.
12. The owner takes a computer from the business for his personal (permanent) use. The Drawings account will receive a _____ entry.

 Name________________________ Date________________

ANSWERS TO SECTION 5.1 EXERCISES (cont.)

Exercise 4, p. 118 (Workbook Exercise)

Shown below is a list of accounts for Alison Morphy, a self-employed photographer.

Bank
Account Receivable—D. Khan
Account Receivable—W. Leroux
Account Receivable—R. Parke
Office Supplies
Photographic Supplies
Equipment
Automobile
Account Payable—Master Chemical Co.
Account Payable—Saddler Photo Service
A. Morphy, Capital
A. Morphy, Drawings
Revenue
Car Expense
Miscellaneous Expense
Rent Expense
Wages Expense

Record the accounting entries for the transactions below in the schedule provided below.

Transactions

June

5 Received $40 cash from M. Tyler who came to the studio for passport photos.
9 Issued a cheque for $95 to Prince Motors for repairs to the car.
12 Issued a cheque for $500 to Milrig Investments for the rent for the month.
17 Issued a bill for $450 to Ross Parke for wedding photos taken on account.
20 Received a bill from Master Chemical Co. regarding the purchase of $350 of photographic supplies on account.
25 Issued a cheque for $24.75 for the monthly telephone bill, paid by cash.
25 Issued a cheque to the owner for $400 for her personal use.
27 Issued a cheque for $355 to West End Garage. The payment was as directed by the owner for the repairs to the owner's husband's car.

DATE	DEBITS		CREDITS	
	ACCOUNT(S)	AMOUNT	ACCOUNT(S)	AMOUNT

 Name ____________ Date ____________

ANSWERS TO SECTION 5.1 EXERCISES (cont.)

Exercise 5, p. 118 Ace Repair Solutions Chart

No.	Asset		Liability		Revenue (Equity) (Increase)	Expense (Equity) (Decrease)	Drawings (Equity) (Decrease)
	Increase	Decrease	Decrease	Increase			
1.	✔				✔		
2.							
3.							
4.							
5.							
6.							
7.							
8.							
9.							
10.							

 Name________________ Date________________

ANSWERS TO SECTION 5.2 REVIEW QUESTIONS (text, p. 125)

Completing Ledger Theory

1. ____________________

2. ____________________

3. ____________________

4. ____________________

5. ____________________

6. ____________________

7. ____________________

8. ____________________

9. ____________________

Chapter 5

Name________________ Date________________

ANSWERS TO SECTION 5.2 EXERCISES (text, p. 125)

Exercise 1, p. 125

Using the table below, complete the exercise that follows.

1.	Asset debit
2.	Asset credit
3.	Liability debit
4.	Liability credit
5.	Capital debit
6.	Capital credit
7.	Drawings debit
8.	Drawings credit
9.	Revenue debit
10.	Revenue credit
11.	Expense debit
12.	Expense credit

A series of transactions is given below. Show the effect of the accounting entry for each transaction. The first transaction is done for you.

Transaction		
1. Purchase a new car on account.	1	4
2. Receive payment on account from a customer.		
3. Owner withdraws cash for personal use.		
4. Owner starts a new business by investing cash.		
5. The car is repaired and paid for in cash immediately.		
6. Perform a service for a customer for cash.		
7. Perform a service for a customer on account.		
8. Purchase supplies for cash.		
9. Receive a bill for gas and oil for the car.		
10. Pay a creditor on account.		
11. Throw out some ruined supplies.		

 Name ________________________ Date ________________

ANSWERS TO SECTION 5.2 EXERCISES (cont.)

Exercise 2, p. 126

1.

____

____

____

			DEBIT	CREDIT

ANSWERS TO SECTION 5.2 EXERCISES (cont.)

Ex. 2 (cont.)

2.

E. Stokaluk
Chart of Accounts

 Name ____________ Date ____________

ANSWERS TO SECTION 5.2 EXERCISES (cont.)

Ex. 2 (cont.)

3.

 Name ______________ Date ______________

ANSWERS TO SECTION 5.2 EXERCISES (cont.)

Exercise 3, p. 127

1., 2.

Karen's Air Service
Chart of Accounts

Exercise 4, p. 127

A	=	L	+	OE	
Assets		Liabilities		Capital	Revenue
DEBIT / CREDIT		DEBIT / CREDIT		DEBIT / CREDIT	DEBIT / CREDIT
				Drawings	Expense
				DEBIT / CREDIT	DEBIT / CREDIT

ANSWERS TO SECTION 5.2 EXERCISES (cont.)

Exercise 5, p. 128

Chapter 5

Name________________ Date________________

ANSWERS TO SECTION 5.2 EXERCISES (cont.)

Exercise 6, p. 128

Complete the following schedule for each of the five separate equity section relationships.

	1.	2.	3.	4.	5.
Beginning capital	6	6	15		62
Total revenues	10		29		
Total expenses	8	11		30	35
Net income or loss (–)		14	11	20	–5
Drawings	3	12		15	
Increase or decrease (–) in equity			–6		–10
Ending capital				10	

 Name____________________ Date________________

ANSWERS TO COMPUTER REVIEW 5.3 QUESTIONS (text, p. 131)

Using Spreadsheets Efficiently

1. ____
2. ____
3. ____
4. ____
5. ____

Communicate It (text, p. 131)

Chapter 5

Name____________________ Date________________

ANSWERS TO CHAPTER 5 EXERCISES (text, p. 132)

USING YOUR KNOWLEDGE

Exercise 1, p. 132

ACCOUNT	NORMAL BALANCE
Supplies	________
Advertising Expense	________
A. Bryce, Drawings	________
G. Wright, a creditor	________
Rent Expense	________
Fees Earned	________
Bank Loan	________
W. Magill, a debtor	________
A. Bryce, Capital	________
Mortgage Payable	________
Automobile	________

Exercise 2, p. 133

1. ____
____

2. ____

ANSWERS TO CHAPTER 5 EXERCISES (cont.)

Exercise 3, p. 133

ANSWERS TO CHAPTER 5 EXERCISES (cont.)

Exercise 4, p. 133

1.

Bank	
1 745	

A.R. – P. Adler	
50	

A.R. – A. Jackson	
70	

Equipment	
5 000	

Supplies	
610	

Automobile	
7 900	

A.P. – Century Finance	
	5 500

A.P. – B & B Store	
	110

P. Garside, Capital	
	5 625

P. Garside, Drawings	
200	

Revenue	
	11 920

Car Expense	
500	

Light, Heat, Water	
280	

Rent	
300	

Wages	
6 500	

	DEBITS		CREDITS	
No.	ACCOUNT(S)	AMOUNT	ACCOUNT(S)	AMOUNT
a				
b				
c				
d				

2. The corrected net income figure will be ______.

ANSWERS TO CHAPTER 5 EXERCISES (cont.)

Exercise 5, p. 134

	Assets	=	Liabilities	+	Beginning Capital	+	Revenue	–	Expenses	–	Drawings.
End of											
Year 1	100	=	20	+	70	+	60	–	45	–	5
Year 2	120	=	30	+		+	90	–	60	–	
Year 3	130	=		+		+	105	–	80	–	20
Year 4		=	30	+		+	110	–	95	–	10

Exercise 6, p. 134

	Assets	*Liabilities*	*Equity*
End of 19–1		$27 400	
End of 19–2			$19 300

 Name______________________ Date______________

ANSWERS TO CHAPTER 5 EXERCISES (cont.)

COMPREHENSIVE EXERCISE

Exercise 7, p. 135

No.	DEBITS		CREDITS	
	ACCOUNT	AMOUNT	ACCOUNT	AMOUNT

 Name________________ Date________________

ANSWERS TO CHAPTER 5 EXERCISES (cont.)

Ex. 7 (cont.)

Bank

Account Receivable
Jenkins and Co.

Office Supplies

Office Equipment

Automobile

Account Payable
Office Supply Company

N.A. James, Capital

N.A. James, Drawings

Fees Earned

Advertising Expense

Car Expense

Donations Expense

Miscellaneous Expense

Rent Expense

 Name________________________ Date____________________

ANSWERS TO CHAPTER 5 EXERCISES (cont.)

Ex. 7 (cont.)

 Name________________ Date____________

ANSWERS TO CHAPTER 5 EXERCISES (cont.)

Ex. 7 (cont.)

 Name________________ Date________________

ANSWERS TO CHAPTER 5 EXERCISES (cont.)

FOR FURTHER THOUGHT

Exercise 8, p. 136

1. ________________

2. ________________

3. ________________

4. ________________

5. ________________

6. ________________

7. ________________

8. ________________

9. ________________
   a. ________________
   b. ________________
   c. ________________
   d. ________________
   e. ________________
   f. ________________

10. ________________

11. ________________

12. ________________

13. ________________

 Name________________ Date________________

ANSWERS TO CHAPTER 5 EXERCISES (cont.)

Exercise 8, p. 136

14. ________________

15. ________________

CASE STUDIES (text, p. 137)

Case 1 *Analyzing an Income Statement Covering Two Years*, p. 137

Part A

1. ________________
2. ________________
3. ________________
4. ________________

Part B

Chapter 5

Name________________________ Date__________________

CASE STUDIES (cont.)

Case 2 *Studying Results of Operation*, p. 138

1.

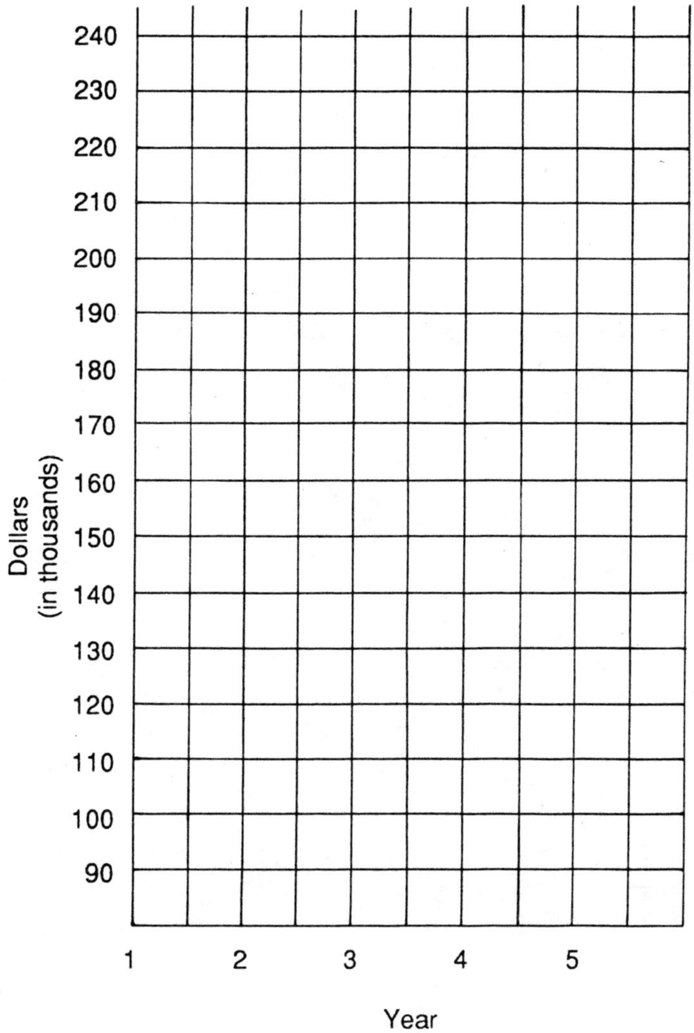

2. ____

3. ____

4. ____

5. ____

CASE STUDIES (cont.)

Case 3 *Perspective on Financial Statements*, p. 139

1. ______________________________

2. ______________________________

3. ______________________________

4. ______________________________

5. ______________________________

6. ______________________________

7. ______________________________

8. ______________________________

Case 4 *Analyzing the Records of a Business*, p. 140

1. a. In 19–4 ______________________________

b. ______________________________

c. ______________________________

CASE STUDIES (cont.)

Case 4, (cont.)

2. a. In 19–5

b.

c.

d.

3. a. In 19–6

b.

c.

d.

Chapter 5

Name________________________ Date________________

CAREER Robert Hunt, CMA/Intermediate Accountant

ANSWERS TO DISCUSSION QUESTIONS (text, p. 143)

1.

2.

3.

4.

5.

6.

7.

 Name______________ Date______________

Chapter 6 The Journal and Source Documents

ANSWERS TO SECTION 6.1 REVIEW QUESTIONS (text, p. 148)

The Journal

1. ______________________________

2. ______________________________

3. ______________________________

4. ______________________________

5. ______________________________

6. ______________________________

7.

8. ______________________________

9. ______________________________

10. ______________________________

11. ______________________________

12. ______________________________

13. ______________________________

14. ______________________________

15. ______________________________

ANSWERS TO SECTION 6.1 EXERCISES (text, p. 148)

Exercise 1, p. 148

GENERAL JOURNAL

PAGE ______

DATE		PARTICULARS	P.R.	DEBIT	CREDIT

ANSWERS TO SECTION 6.1 EXERCISES (cont.)

Ex. 1 (cont.)

GENERAL JOURNAL PAGE ______

DATE		PARTICULARS	P.R.	DEBIT	CREDIT

Exercise 2, p. 149

1.

____

____

____

ANSWERS TO SECTION 6.1 EXERCISES (cont.)

Ex. 2 (cont.)

2.

GENERAL JOURNAL

PAGE ______

DATE		PARTICULARS	P.R.	DEBIT	CREDIT

 Name ______________ Date ______________

ANSWERS TO SECTION 6.1 EXERCISES (cont.)

Ex. 2 (cont.)

3.

GENERAL JOURNAL

PAGE ______

DATE		PARTICULARS	P.R.	DEBIT	CREDIT

ANSWERS TO SECTION 6.1 EXERCISES (cont.)

Exercise 3, p. 150

1. ____________
2. ____________
3. ____________
4. ____________
5. ____________
6. ____________
7. ____________
8. ____________

Exercise 4, p. 151

Transaction 1

____

Transaction 2

____

Transaction 3

____

Transaction 4

____

Transaction 5

____

Exercise 5, p. 151

GENERAL JOURNAL PAGE ______

DATE		PARTICULARS	P.R.	DEBIT	CREDIT

Chapter 6

Name ____________________ Date ____________________

ANSWERS TO SECTION 6.1 EXERCISES (cont.)

Exercise 6, p. 151

GENERAL JOURNAL

PAGE ________

DATE 19 – 5		PARTICULARS	P.R.	DEBIT	CREDIT

 Name________________________ Date________________

ANSWERS TO SECTION 6.2 REVIEW QUESTIONS (text, p. 162)

Source Documents

1. ______________________________

2. ______________________________

3. ______________________________

4. ______________________________

5. ______________________________

6. ______________________________

7. ______________________________

8. ______________________________

9. ______________________________

10. ______________________________

11. ______________________________

12. ______________________________

13. ______________________________

14. ______________________________

15. ______________________________

16. ______________________________

17. ______________________________

18. ______________________________

19. ______________________________

 Name ______________ Date ______________

ANSWERS TO SECTION 6.2 REVIEW QUESTIONS (cont.)

20. ______________

21. ______________

22. ______________

23. ______________

24. ______________

ANSWERS TO SECTION 6.2 EXERCISES (text, p. 163)

Exercise 1, p. 163

1. ______________
2. ______________
3. ______________
4. ______________
5. ______________
6. ______________
7. ______________

Exercise 2, p. 163

1. ______________
2. ______________
3. ______________
4. ______________

ANSWERS TO SECTION 6.2 EXERCISES (cont.)

Ex. 2 (cont.)

5. ______

Exercise 3, p. 164

1. ______

2. ______

3. ______

4. ______

5. ______

Exercise 4, p. 165

1. ______

2. ______

3. ______

4. ______

5. ______

6. ______

7. ______

Exercise 5, p. 166

1. ______

2. ______

3. ______

Chapter 6

Name______________________ Date______________________

ANSWERS TO SECTION 6.3 REVIEW QUESTIONS (text, p. 170)

Sales Tax

1. ______________________

2. ______________________

3. ______________________

4. ______________________
   1) ______________________
   2) ______________________
   3) ______________________
   4) ______________________

5. ______________________

6. ______________________

7. ______________________

8. ______________________

ANSWERS TO SECTION 6.3 EXERCISES (text, p. 170)

Exercise 1, p. 170

1. 1. ______________________
   2. ______________________
   3. ______________________
   4. ______________________
   5. ______________________

2. 1. ______________________
   2. ______________________
   3. ______________________
   4. ______________________
   5. ______________________

 Name ______________ Date ______________

ANSWERS TO SECTION 6.3 EXERCISES (cont.)

Ex. 1 (cont.)

3.

GENERAL JOURNAL

PAGE ______

DATE		PARTICULARS	P.R.	DEBIT	CREDIT
	a)				
	b)				
	c)				
	d)				
	e)				

 Name ______________________ Date ______________________

ANSWERS TO SECTION 6.3 EXERCISES (cont.)

Exercise 2, p. 170

1., 2.

GENERAL JOURNAL

PAGE ________

DATE		PARTICULARS	P.R.	DEBIT	CREDIT
1.					
2.					

ANSWERS TO SECTION 6.3 EXERCISES (cont.)

Exercise 3, p. 171

1. ____________________

2. ____________________

3. ____________________

Exercise 4, p. 171

1. ____________________

2. ____________________

3. ____________________

4. ____________________

5. ____________________

6. ____________________

 Name ______________________ Date ________________

ANSWERS TO SECTION 6.3 EXERCISES (cont.)

Exercise 5, p. 172

1.

MOORE'S MARINA

16 Harbourfront Rd.
Vancouver, B.C.
V7C 8T8
Phone 888-6666

Date __________ 19____

Name ____

Address ______________________________________

Qty	Description	Price	Amount	
RECEIVED ABOVE IN GOOD ORDER		Tax		
		Total		

Cash	Charge

SALES SLIP 9124

2. ____

____

____

____

Chapter 6

Name____________________ Date________________

ANSWERS TO CHAPTER 6 EXERCISES (text, p. 173)

USING YOUR KNOWLEDGE

Exercise 1, p. 173

a. ____________________
b. ____________________
c. ____________________
d. ____________________
e. ____________________
f. ____________________
g. ____________________
h. ____________________
i. ____________________
j. ____________________
k. ____________________
l. ____________________

Exercise 2, p. 173

Complete the following summary.

Nature of Transaction	Source Document or Documents	The Required Journal Entry	
		Account Debited	Account Credited
Payment on Account			
Sale on Account			
Bank Service Charge			
Cash Payment of Phone Bill			
Cash Received on Account			
Puchase of Equipment on Account			
Cash Sale			

 Name________________________ Date__________________

ANSWERS TO CHAPTER 6 EXERCISES (cont.)

Exercise 3, p. 174

Source Document	Document Number
Bank Credit Memo	*1.*
Bank Debit Memo	*2.*
Cheque Copy	*3.*
Cash Sales Slip	*4.*
Sales Invoice	*5.*
Purchase Invoice	*6.*
Receipt Invoice	*7.*
Cash Receipts List	*8.*
Owner's Written Memo	*9.*
Sales Slip Received	*10.*
Bank Statement	*11.*

Transactions	Document Number
1. Owner withdraws money.	
2. Purchase of equipment on account.	
3. Payment on account.	
4. Cash sale.	
5. Cash payment for donation.	
6. Purchase of office supplies by cash.	
7. Sale on account.	
8. Cheques received from customers on account.	
9. Increase bank loan.	
10. Owner invests additional money in the business.	
11. Bank service charge.	

Exercise 4, p. 174

For each of the following statements indicate whether it is true or false by placing a "T" or "F" in the space provided. For each "F" response explain why you believe that the statement is false.

1. Anyone in the business can initiate a business transaction. ☐
2. Every journal entry is based on a source document. ☐
3. The only purpose of source documents is to provide the basis for a journal entry. ☐
4. A business that sells to its customers on a cash basis would not normally use a sales invoice. ☐
5. The journal entry for all cash sales slips is essentially the same. ☐
6. Sales invoices are used by businesses that make most of their sales on account. ☐
7. For every sales invoice there is a debit to an account receivable. ☐
8. Dual purpose sales slips are the choice of businesses that sell for cash and also on account. ☐
9. Every sales invoice is also a purchase invoice. ☐
10. The debit entry for every purchase invoice is always the same. ☐

ANSWERS TO CHAPTER 6 EXERCISES (cont.)

Ex. 4 (cont.)

11. The supporting document for a payment on account is the tear-off portion of a cheque. ☐

12. The credit entry for every cheque copy payment is always the same. ☐

13. Cheques received are considered to be cash received. ☐

14. The bank has no right to make deductions from the accounts of its customers. ☐

15. We debit Bank when we receive a bank debit memo. ☐

16. The cost principle states that every acquisition of assets is to be recorded at their cost price. ☐

17. The best objective evidence of a purchase is a purchase invoice received at "arm's length." ☐

18. Only provincial governments are allowed to levy retail sales taxes. ☐

19. The purchaser of goods or services is required to make accounting entries for sales tax. ☐

20. The Sales Tax account is an expense account. ☐

Explanations

____

____

____

____

____

____

____

____

____

____

____

 Name ______________ Date ______________

ANSWERS TO CHAPTER 6 EXERCISES (cont.)

COMPREHENSIVE EXERCISES

Exercise 5, p. 175

GENERAL JOURNAL PAGE ______

DATE		PARTICULARS	P.R.	DEBIT	CREDIT

 Name ____________ Date ____________

ANSWERS TO CHAPTER 6 EXERCISES (cont.)

Ex. 5 (cont.)

GENERAL JOURNAL

PAGE ______

DATE		PARTICULARS	P.R.	DEBIT	CREDIT

ANSWERS TO CHAPTER 6 EXERCISES (cont.)

Exercise 6, p. 176

GENERAL JOURNAL

PAGE ______

DATE	Accounts	Debit	Credit

 Name____________________ Date____________

ANSWERS TO CHAPTER 6 EXERCISES (cont.)

Ex. 6 (cont.)

GENERAL JOURNAL

PAGE ________

DATE	Accounts	Debit	Credit

 Name________________ Date________________

ANSWERS TO CHAPTER 6 EXERCISES (cont.)

Exercise 7, p. 177 **GENERAL JOURNAL** PAGE ________

DATE	Accounts	Debit	Credit

ANSWERS TO CHAPTER 6 EXERCISES (cont.)

Ex. 7 (cont.) **GENERAL JOURNAL** **PAGE** ________

DATE	Accounts	Debit	Credit

ANSWERS TO CHAPTER 6 EXERCISES (cont.)

Exercise 8, p. 178

1. ______
2. ______
3. ______
4. ______
5. ______
6. ______

FOR FURTHER THOUGHT

Exercise 9, p. 179

1. ______
2. ______
3. ______
4. ______
5. ______
6. ______
7. ______
8. ______
9. ______

ANSWERS TO CHAPTER 6 EXERCISES (cont.)

Ex. 9 (cont.)

10. ____

____

____

11. ____

____

____

____

12. ____

____

Chapter 6

Name________________________ Date________________

CASE STUDIES (text, p. 179)

Case 1 *Acquiring Assets in a Package Deal*, p. 179

1. ____________________

2. ____________________

3. ____________________

4. ____________________

5. ____________________

6. ____________________

Case 2 *Is a Profit Always a Profit?*, p. 180

1. ____________________

2. ____________________

3. ____________________

CASE STUDIES (cont.)

Case 2 (cont.)

4. ______________________________

5. ______________________________

6. ______________________________

7. ______________________________

8. ______________________________

Case 3 *Profit before Sentiment?*, p. 181

1. ______________________________

2. ______________________________

3. ______________________________

4. ______________________________

Chapter 6

Name____________________ Date________________

CAREER Barbara Blaney, CA/Public Accountant

ANSWERS TO DISCUSSION QUESTIONS (text, p. 183)

1.

2.

3.

4.

5.

6.

7.

8.

9.

 Name________________ Date________________

Chapter 7 Posting

ANSWERS TO SECTION 7.1 REVIEW QUESTIONS (text, p. 195)

Posting

1. ________________

2. ________________

3. ________________

____

4. ________________

5. ________________

____

6. ________________

7. ________________

8. ________________

1) ________________

2) ________________

3) ________________

4) ________________

5) ________________

9. ________________

____

10. ________________

____

11. 1. ________________

2. ________________

3. ________________

12. ________________

____

13. ________________

14. ________________

____

15. ________________

1) ________________

2) ________________

3) ________________

4) ________________

ANSWERS TO SECTION 7.1 EXERCISES (text, p. 195)

Exercise 1, p. 195

A. Asset

Debit	Credit	Balance D/C	Balance Amount
1 000 00			
250 00			
310 00			
	1 250 00		
200 00			
350 00			
	860 00		
850 00			
	1 000 00		
1 500 00			
200 00			

B. Liability

Debit	Credit	Balance D/C	Balance Amount
	3 500 00		
	1 600 00		
3 500 00			
1 000 00			
	2 000 00		
600 00			
2 000 00			
	450 00		
500 00			
	50 00		
	375 00		

 Name______ Date______

ANSWERS TO SECTION 7.1 EXERCISES (text, p. 195)

Exercise 2, p. 196 (Workbook Exercise)

The journal and ledger of C. Fries appear below and on the next pages. Post the journal entries to the ledger accounts. When this is completed take off a trial balance to ensure that your work is accurate.

GENERAL JOURNAL

PAGE 40

DATE 19—		PARTICULARS	P.R.	DEBIT	CREDIT
Jan.	4	Bank		700 –	
		Revenue			700 –
		Cash Sale			
	7	Wages		1 500 –	
		Bank			1 500 –
		Wages for Brown & Ross			
	10	Bank		300 –	
		A/R — P. Berry			300 –
		Received on account			
	15	Supplies		1 110 –	
		A/P — General Supply Co.			1 110 –
		Paper products			
	21	A/R — P. Berry		500 –	
		Revenue			500 –
		Sale on account			
	25	C. Fries, Drawings		750 –	
		Bank			750 –
		Personal use			
	30	General Expense		40 –	
		Bank			40 –
		Materials used			

ANSWERS TO SECTION 7.1 EXERCISES (cont.)

Ex. 2 (cont.)

ACCOUNT Bank **NO.** 101

DATE 19 —		PARTICULARS	P.R.	DEBIT	CREDIT	D/C	BALANCE
Jan.	1					DR	1 375 –

ACCOUNT A/R — P. Berry **NO.** 105

DATE 19 —		PARTICULARS	P.R.	DEBIT	CREDIT	D/C	BALANCE
Jan.	1					DR	300 –

ACCOUNT Supplies **NO.** 110

DATE 19 —		PARTICULARS	P.R.	DEBIT	CREDIT	D/C	BALANCE
Jan.	1					DR	950 –

ACCOUNT Equipment **NO.** 115

DATE 19 —		PARTICULARS	P.R.	DEBIT	CREDIT	D/C	BALANCE
Jan.	1					DR	9 450 –

ANSWERS TO SECTION 7.1 EXERCISES (cont.)

Ex. 2 (cont.)

ACCOUNT A/P — General Supply Co. **NO.** 201

DATE 19 —		PARTICULARS	P.R.	DEBIT	CREDIT	D/C	BALANCE
Jan.	1					CR	3 240 –

ACCOUNT C. Fries, Capital **NO.** 301

DATE 19 —		PARTICULARS	P.R.	DEBIT	CREDIT	D/C	BALANCE
Jan.	1					CR	8 835 –

ACCOUNT C. Fries, Drawings **NO.** 302

DATE 19 —		PARTICULARS	P.R.	DEBIT	CREDIT	D/C	BALANCE

ACCOUNT Revenue **NO.** 401

DATE 19 —		PARTICULARS	P.R.	DEBIT	CREDIT	D/C	BALANCE

ACCOUNT General Expense **NO.** 505

DATE 19 —		PARTICULARS	P.R.	DEBIT	CREDIT	D/C	BALANCE

 Name________________ Date________________

ANSWERS TO SECTION 7.1 EXERCISES (cont.)

Ex. 2 (cont.)

ACCOUNT Wages **NO.** 510

DATE 19 —		PARTICULARS	P.R.	DEBIT	CREDIT	D/C	BALANCE

 Name______________________ Date________________

ANSWERS TO SECTION 7.1 EXERCISES (cont.)

Exercise 3, p. 196

The journal and the ledger of Pauline Jacobs appear below and on the following pages. Post the journal entries to the ledger accounts. When this is completed, take off a trial balance.

GENERAL JOURNAL

PAGE 18

DATE 19 —		PARTICULARS	P.R.	DEBIT	CREDIT
Sept.	3	Automobile Expense		75 –	
		Bank			75 –
		Car repair paid by cheque			
	5	Bank		1500 –	
		A/R — R. Todd			1500 –
		Received on account			
	7	Supplies		650 –	
		A/P — U-Call-Us			650 –
		Supplies on account			
	10	Bank		900 –	
		Revenue			900 –
		Service for cash			
	10	Wages		1200 –	
		Bank			1200 –
		For week ended			
	11	General Expense		1000 –	
		Bank			1000 –
		Rent for month			
	13	Bank		800 –	
		Revenue			800 –
		Service for cash			
	15	Pauline Jacobs, Drawings		300 –	
		Bank			300 –
		For personal use			

ANSWERS TO SECTION 7.1 EXERCISES (cont.)

Ex. 3 (cont.)

ACCOUNT Bank **NO.** 101

DATE 19 —		PARTICULARS	P.R.	DEBIT	CREDIT	D/C	BALANCE
Aug.	31					DR	8 516 –

ACCOUNT A/R — R. Todd **NO.** 110

DATE 19 —		PARTICULARS	P.R.	DEBIT	CREDIT	D/C	BALANCE
Aug.	31					DR	3 750 –

ACCOUNT Supplies **NO.** 120

DATE 19 —		PARTICULARS	P.R.	DEBIT	CREDIT	D/C	BALANCE
Aug.	31					DR	900 –

ACCOUNT Automobile **NO.** 130

DATE 19 —		PARTICULARS	P.R.	DEBIT	CREDIT	D/C	BALANCE
Aug.	31					DR	19 406 –

ANSWERS TO SECTION 7.1 EXERCISES (cont.)

Ex. 3 (cont.)

ACCOUNT A/P — U-Call-Us **NO.** 210

DATE 19 —		PARTICULARS	P.R.	DEBIT	CREDIT	D/C	BALANCE
Aug.	31					CR	1 235 –

ACCOUNT Pauline Jacobs, Capital **NO.** 301

DATE 19 —		PARTICULARS	P.R.	DEBIT	CREDIT	D/C	BALANCE
Aug.	31					CR	32 555 –

ACCOUNT Pauline Jacobs, Drawings **NO.** 302

DATE 19 —		PARTICULARS	P.R.	DEBIT	CREDIT	D/C	BALANCE
Aug.	31					DR	10 400 –

ACCOUNT Revenue **NO.** 401

DATE 19 —		PARTICULARS	P.R.	DEBIT	CREDIT	D/C	BALANCE
Aug.	31					CR	40 706 –

ACCOUNT Automobile Expense **NO.** 505

DATE 19 —		PARTICULARS	P.R.	DEBIT	CREDIT	D/C	BALANCE
Aug.	31					DR	5 906 –

 Name______________ Date______________

ANSWERS TO SECTION 7.1 EXERCISES (cont.)

Ex. 3 (cont.)

ACCOUNT General Expense **NO.** 510

DATE 19 —		PARTICULARS	P.R.	DEBIT	CREDIT	D/C	BALANCE
Aug.	31					DR	6215 –

ACCOUNT Wages **NO.** 515

DATE 19 —		PARTICULARS	P.R.	DEBIT	CREDIT	D/C	BALANCE
Aug.	31					DR	19403 –

 Name________________ Date____________

ANSWERS TO SECTION 7.1 EXERCISES (cont.)

Exercise 4, p. 196 (Workbook Exercise)

The Cash account page shown below is filled. Forward the balance to a new account page.

ACCOUNT Cash **NO.** 1

DATE		PARTICULARS	P.R.	DEBIT	CREDIT	DR CR	BALANCE
19 — July	1		J1	1900 –		DR	1900 –
	7		J1	1900 –		DR	3800 –
	13		J1		500 –	DR	3300 –
	19		J2		275 –	DR	3025 –
	21		J2		50 –	DR	2975 –
	25		J2		75 –	DR	2900 –
	27		J3	1000 –		DR	3900 –
	29		J3		100 –	DR	3800 –

ACCOUNT **NO.**

DATE 19 —		PARTICULARS	P.R.	DEBIT	CREDIT	DR CR	BALANCE

Chapter 7

Name ______________________ Date ________________

ANSWERS TO SECTION 7.2 REVIEW QUESTIONS (text, p. 198)

Trial Balance Out of Balance

1. ______________________________
____
____

2. ______________________________
1) ______________________________
2) ______________________________
3) ______________________________
4) ______________________________
5) ______________________________

3. ______________________________
____

4. ______________________________

5. ______________________________

6. ______________________________

7. ______________________________
____

8. ______________________________
____

9. ______________________________
____

ANSWERS TO SECTION 7.2 EXERCISES (text, p. 198)

Exercise 1, p. 198 (Workbook Exercise)

The exercise below, involving a journal, ledger, and trial balance, has errors in it. Locate and make the corrections for all of the errors in the exercise.

GENERAL JOURNAL

PAGE ________

DATE 19 —		PARTICULARS	P.R.	DEBIT	CREDIT
Nov.	4	Bank	1	12 000 –	
		Supplies	3	570 –	
		Furniture	4	1 971 50	
		A. Holmes, Capital	30		14 541 50
		Opening entry			
	5	Automobile	5	4 861 21	
		Bank	1		1 000 –
		Account Payable — Ace Finance Co.	20		3 681 21
		Purchase of new Ford for $4 861.21			
	6	Furniture	4	412 90	
		Bank	1		412 00
		Purchase of new desk for $412.90			
	7	Account Receivable — A. Boyd	2	140 –	
		Revenue	30		140 –
		Service performed on account			
	10	Bank	1	99 90	
		Revenue	30		99 90
		Service performed for cash			
	12	Rent Expense	30	165 –	
		Bank	1		165 –
		Rent paid for month			
	15	Car Expense	30	97 –	
		Bank	1		97 –
		Car repair bill paid — $97.00			
	15	Account payable — Ace Finance Co.	20	214 71	
		Bank	1		214 71
		First instalment paid			

ANSWERS TO SECTION 7.2 EXERCISES (cont.)

Ex. 1 (cont.) **The Ledger**

ACCOUNT Bank **NO.**

DATE 19 —		PARTICULARS	P.R.	DEBIT	CREDIT	DR CR	BALANCE
Nov.	4		J1	12 000 –		DR	12 000 –
	5		J1		100 –	DR	11 900 –
	6		J1		412 –	DR	11 488 –
	10		J1	99 90		DR	11 587 –
	12		J1		165 –	DR	11 422 90
	15		J1		214 71	DR	11 208 19

ACCOUNT Account Receivable — A. Boyd **NO.** 2

DATE 19 —		PARTICULARS	P.R.	DEBIT	CREDIT	DR CR	BALANCE
Nov.	7		J1	140 –		DR	140 –

ACCOUNT Supplies **NO.** 3

DATE 19 —		PARTICULARS	P.R.	DEBIT	CREDIT	DR CR	BALANCE
Nov.	4		J1	570 –		DR	570 –

ACCOUNT Furniture **NO.** 4

DATE 19 —		PARTICULARS	P.R.	DEBIT	CREDIT	DR CR	BALANCE
Nov.	4		J1	1 971 50		DR	1 971 50
	6		J1	412 90		DR	2 384 40

ANSWERS TO SECTION 7.2 EXERCISES (cont.)

Ex. 1 (cont.)

ACCOUNT Automobile **NO.** 5

DATE 19 —		PARTICULARS	P.R.	DEBIT	CREDIT	DR CR	BALANCE
Nov.	5		J1	4 861 21		DR	4 861 21

ACCOUNT Account Payable — Ace Finance Co. **NO.** 20

DATE 19 —		PARTICULARS	P.R.	DEBIT	CREDIT	DR CR	BALANCE
Nov.	5		J1		3 681 21	CR	3 681 21
	15		J1	214 71		CR	3 466 50

ACCOUNT A. Holmes, Capital **NO.** 30

DATE 19 —		PARTICULARS	P.R.	DEBIT	CREDIT	DR CR	BALANCE
Nov.	4		J1		14 541 50	CR	14 541 50

ACCOUNT Revenue **NO.** 40

DATE 19 —		PARTICULARS	P.R.	DEBIT	CREDIT	DR CR	BALANCE
Nov.	7		J1		140 –	CR	140 –
	10		J1		99 90	CR	239 90

ACCOUNT Rent Expense **NO.** 51

DATE 19 —		PARTICULARS	P.R.	DEBIT	CREDIT	DR CR	BALANCE
Nov.	12		J1	165 –		DR	165 –

ACCOUNT Car Expense **NO.** 52

DATE 19 —		PARTICULARS	P.R.	DEBIT	CREDIT	DR CR	BALANCE
Nov.	15		J1	97 –		DR	97 –

ANSWERS TO SECTION 7.2 EXERCISES (cont.)

Ex. 1 (cont.)

A. Holmes

Trial Balance

November 15, 19 —

No.		Account	Debit		Credit	
1		Bank	11 208	19		
2		Account Receivable — A. Boyd			140	–
3		Supplies	750	–		
4		Furniture	2 384	40		
5		Automobile	4 861	21		
20		Account Payable — Ace Finance			3 466	50
30		A. Holmes, Capital			14 541	40
40		Revenue			239	90
51		Rent Expense	165	–		
52		Car Expense	97	–		
			19 465	80	18 387	90

ANSWERS TO SECTION 7.2 EXERCISES (cont.)

Exercise 2, p. 198 (Workbook Exercise)

The exercise below, involving a journal, ledger, and trial balance, contains errors. Locate and make the corrections for all of the errors in the exercise.

GENERAL JOURNAL

PAGE ______

DATE 19 —		PARTICULARS	P.R.	DEBIT	CREDIT
Aug.	1	Bank	1	15 000 –	
		Supplies	3	500 –	
		Furniture	4	790 –	
		R. Wood, Capital	30		16 290 –
		Opening entry			
	5	Automobile	5	5 090 –	
		Bank	1		2 000 –
		A/C Pay'l — George's Motors	20		3 090 –
		New car for sales department, $5 090			
	6	Furniture	4	412 90	
		Bank	1		412 90
		New desk, $412.90			
	8	A/C Rec'l — C. Potter	2	661 26	
		Revenue	40		626 16
		Service performed, $661.26			
	12	Rent Expense	51	175 –	
		Bank	1		170 –
		Monthly Rent, $170.			
	13	Car Expense	50	57 42	
		R. Wood, Drawings	31	200 –	
		Bank	1		257 42
		Bill for car repairs, $257.42			
	15	Bank	1	385 –	
		Revenue	40		385 –
		Service performed, $385.			

ANSWERS TO SECTION 7.2 EXERCISES (cont.)

Ex. 2 (cont.)

GENERAL JOURNAL

PAGE ______

DATE 19—		PARTICULARS	P.R.	DEBIT	CREDIT
Aug.	15	A/C Pay'l — George's Motors	20	300 –	
		Bank	1		300 –
		Instalment payment, $300			
	16	Supplies	3	240 –	
		Bank	1		240 –
		Various office supplies, $240			

ANSWERS TO SECTION 7.2 EXERCISES (cont.)

Ex. 2 (cont.)

ACCOUNT Bank **NO.** 1

DATE 19 —		PARTICULARS	P.R.	DEBIT	CREDIT	DR CR	BALANCE
Aug.	1		J1	15 000 –		DR	15 000 –
	5		J1		2 000 –	DR	13 000 –
	6		J1		412 90	DR	12 587 10
	12		J1		170 –	DR	12 417 10
	13		J1		257 42	DR	12 159 68
	15		J1	385 –		DR	12 544 68
	15		J1		300 –	DR	12 244 68
	16		J1		240 –	DR	12 004 68

ACCOUNT Account Receivable — C. Potter **NO.** 2

DATE 19 —		PARTICULARS	P.R.	DEBIT	CREDIT	DR CR	BALANCE
Aug.	8		J1	661 26		DR	661 26

ACCOUNT Supplies **NO.** 3

DATE 19 —		PARTICULARS	P.R.	DEBIT	CREDIT	DR CR	BALANCE
Aug.	1		J1	500 –		DR	500 –
	16		J1	240 –		DR	840 –

ACCOUNT Furniture **NO.** 4

DATE 19 —		PARTICULARS	P.R.	DEBIT	CREDIT	DR CR	BALANCE
Aug.	1		J1	790 –		DR	790 –
	6		J1	421 90		DR	1 211 90

ANSWERS TO SECTION 7.2 EXERCISES (cont.)

Ex. 2 (cont.)

ACCOUNT Automobile **NO.** 5

DATE 19 —		PARTICULARS	P.R.	DEBIT	CREDIT	DR CR	BALANCE
Aug.	5		J1	5 090 –		DR	5 090 –

ACCOUNT Account Payable — George's Motors **NO.** 20

DATE 19 —		PARTICULARS	P.R.	DEBIT	CREDIT	DR CR	BALANCE
Aug.	5		J1		3 090 –	CR	3 090 –

ACCOUNT R. Wood, Capital **NO.** 30

DATE 19 —		PARTICULARS	P.R.	DEBIT	CREDIT	DR CR	BALANCE
Aug.	1		J1		16 290 –	CR	16 290 –

ACCOUNT R. Wood, Drawings **NO.** 31

DATE 19 —		PARTICULARS	P.R.	DEBIT	CREDIT	DR CR	BALANCE
Aug.	13		J1	200 –		DR	200 –

ACCOUNT Revenue **NO.** 40

DATE 19 —		PARTICULARS	P.R.	DEBIT	CREDIT	DR CR	BALANCE
Aug.	8		J1		626 16	CR	626 16
	15		J1		385 –	CR	1 011 16

ANSWERS TO SECTION 7.2 EXERCISES (cont.)

Ex. 2 (cont.)

ACCOUNT Car Expense **NO.** 50

DATE 19 —		PARTICULARS	P.R.	DEBIT	CREDIT	DR CR	BALANCE
Aug.	13		J1	57 42		DR	57 42

ACCOUNT Rent Expense **NO.** 51

DATE 19 —		PARTICULARS	P.R.	DEBIT	CREDIT	DR CR	BALANCE
Aug.	12		J1	175 –		DR	175 –

R. Wood

Trial Balance

August 16, 19 —

No.			DEBIT	CREDIT
1		Bank	12 004 68	
2		Acc. Rec'l — C. Potter	661 26	
3		Supplies	840 –	
4		Furniture	1 211 90	
5		Automobile	5 090 –	
20		Acc. Pay'l — George's Motors		3 090 –
30		R. Wood, Capital		16 290 –
31		R. Wood, Drawings	200 –	
40		Revenue		1 011 16
50		Car Expense	57 42	
			20 065 26	20 391 16

ANSWERS TO SECTION 7.2 EXERCISES (cont.)

Exercise 3, p. 199

1. **Why does it not balance?**

JOURNAL

PARTICULARS	DR	CR
Bank	4 500	
Equipment	3 600	
Capital		8 100
Supplies	73	
Accounts Payable		73
Expense	47	
Bank		47
Bank	195	
Revenue		195
Drawings	100	
Bank		100
Accounts Receivable	63	
Revenue		63
Supplies	38	
Bank		38

LEDGER

Bank

DR	CR
4 500	47
195	100
	38
(4 510) 4 695	185

Accounts Receivable

DR	CR
63	

Supplies

DR	CR
73	
38	
111	

Equipment

DR	CR
3 600	

Accounts Payable

DR	CR
	73

Capital

DR	CR
	8 100

Drawings

DR	CR
100	

Revenue

DR	CR
	159
	63
	222

Expense

DR	CR
47	

TRIAL BALANCE

DR	CR
4 510	73
63	8 100
111	222
3 600	
100	
47	
8 431	8 395

ANSWERS TO SECTION 7.2 EXERCISES (cont.)

Ex. 3 (cont.)

2. **Why does it not balance?**

JOURNAL

PARTICULARS	DR	CR
Bank	3 000	
Equipment	2 000	
Capital		5 000
Supplies	490	
Bank		490
Accounts Receivable	155	
Revenue		155
Expense	56	
Bank		56
Expense	72	
Accounts Payable		72
Bank	312	
Revenue		312
Drawings	97	
Bank		97

LEDGER

Bank

	Dr	Cr
	3 000	490
	312	56
		97
(2 669)	3 312	643

Accounts Receivab

Dr	Cr
155	

Supplies

Dr	Cr
490	

Equipment

Dr	Cr
2 000	

Accounts Payable

Dr	Cr
	72

Capital

Dr	Cr
	5 000

Drawings

Dr	Cr
97	

Revenue

Dr	Cr
	155
	312
	467

Expense

Dr	Cr
56	

TRIAL BALANC

DR	CR
2 669	72
155	5 000
490	467
2 000	
97	
56	
5 467	5 539

____

____

ANSWERS TO SECTION 7.2 EXERCISES (cont.)

Ex. 3 (cont.)

3. Why does it not balance?

JOURNAL

PARTICULARS	DR	CR
Bank	2 500	
Equipment	7 000	
Capital		9 500
Accounts Receivable	371	
Revenue		371
Bank	269	
Revenue		269
Supplies	53	
Accounts Payable		53
Drawings	127	
Bank		127
Expense	86	
Bank		86
Expense	49	
Accounts Payable		49

LEDGER

Bank (balance: 2 556)

DR	CR
2 500	127
269	86
2 769	213

Accounts Receivable

DR	CR
371	

Supplies

DR	CR
53	

Equipment

DR	CR
7 000	

Accounts Payable

DR	CR
	53
	49
	102

Capital

DR	CR
	9 500

Drawings

DR	CR
127	

Revenue

DR	CR
	371
	269
	540

Expense

DR	CR
86	
49	
135	

TRIAL BALANCE

DR	CR
2 556	102
371	9 500
53	540
7 000	
127	
135	
10 242	10 142

ANSWERS TO SECTION 7.2 EXERCISES (cont.)

Ex. 3 (cont.)

4. **Why does it not balance?**

JOURNAL

PARTICULARS	DR	CR
Bank	4 000	
Equipment	3 000	
Capital		7 000
Supplies	216	
Accounts Payable		216
Accounts Receivable	321	
Revenue		321
Expense	73	
Bank		73
Expense	34	
Accounts Payable		34
Drawings	41	
Bank		41
Bank	150	
Accounts Receivable		150

LEDGER

Bank

DR	CR
4 000	73
150	41
(4 036) 4 150	114

Accounts Receivable

DR	CR
321	150
(171)	

Supplies

DR	CR
216	

Equipment

DR	CR
3 000	

Accounts Payable

DR	CR
	216
	34
	250

Capital

DR	CR
	7 000

Drawings

DR	CR
41	

Revenue

DR	CR
	321

Expense

DR	CR
73	
34	
107	

TRIAL BALANCE

DR	CR
4 036	250
171	7 000
216	41
3 000	321
107	
7 530	7 612

Chapter 7

Name________________________ Date__________________

ANSWERS TO COMPUTER REVIEW 7.3 QUESTIONS (text, p. 209)

1. ____

2. ____

3. ____

4. ____

5. ____

6. ____

7. ____

8. ____

9. ____

10. ____

11. ____

12. ____

13. ____

14. ____

15. ____

16. ____

17. ____

18. ____

 Name________________ Date____________

ANSWERS TO CHAPTER 7 EXERCISES (text, p. 210)

Exercise 1, p. 210

Indicate whether each of the following statements is true or false by placing a "T" or an "F" in the space indicated. Explain the reason for each "F" response in the space provided.

1. The chief advantage of the three-column account is that there is room for the account balance. ☐
2. Both sides of an account page (front and back) are used for the same item, for example, Bank. ☐
3. Entering the journal page number in the account is the sixth step in the posting process. ☐
4. The step described in 3 above is performed in the journal. ☐
5. The process of setting up an account is known as "forwarding." ☐
6. The fourth step in the accounting cycle, as we know it, is the taking off of a trial balance. ☐
7. It is not possible for the ledger to be out of balance and also to be correct. ☐
8. If the trial balance difference is an even amount, the error could not be a transposition error. ☐
9. If the trial balance difference is zero, the ledger is in balance. ☐
10. Posting a debit item incorrectly as a credit produces a trial balance credit total that is smaller than the debit total by twice the amount of the error. ☐
11. Only very rarely does a transaction affect only one account. ☐
12. Ledger accounts are arranged alphabetically to make them easier to find. ☐
13. The presence of the account number in the journal indicates that the posting of an item has been completed. ☐

Explanations

 Name________________ Date____________

ANSWERS TO CHAPTER 7 EXERCISES (cont.)

Ex. 1 (cont.)

____

____

____

Exercise 2, p. 211

Error Situations	Trial Balance Will Not Balance		Trial balance will balance but will not be correct
	Debits greater than Credits by ($$)	Credits greater than Debits by ($$)	
1. An entire journal entry is posted as $400 instead of $100.			
2. A debit of $200 is posted twice.			
3. A debit of $150 is posted as a credit.			
4. The Bank account is over-added by $80.			
5. The Drawings account balance of $5 500 is missed when preparing the trial balance.			
6. The Revenue account balance of $72 000 is listed on the trial balance as a debit.			
7. An entire general journal entry for $325 is not posted.			
8. An entire general journal entry for $50 is posted in reverse.			
9. A $40 debit is not posted.			
10. A $500 credit is posted as $50.			
11. A debit of $60 to Bank was posted to a customer's account.			
12. A $40 debit is posted as $400.			

 Name______________ Date______________

ANSWERS TO CHAPTER 7 EXERCISES (cont.)

Exercise 3, p. 212

Possible errors that would not cause the trial balance to be out of balance:

Exercise 4, p. 212

Exercise 5, p. 212

Exercise 6, p. 212

 Name________________ Date________________

ANSWERS TO CHAPTER 7 EXERCISES (cont.)

COMPREHENSIVE EXERCISE

Exercise 7, p. 212

1., 2.

GENERAL JOURNAL PAGE ______

DATE 19 —		PARTICULARS	P.R.	DEBIT	CREDIT

 Name________________ Date________________

ANSWERS TO CHAPTER 7 EXERCISES (cont.)

Ex. 7 (cont.)

GENERAL JOURNAL

PAGE ______

DATE 19—		PARTICULARS	P.R.	DEBIT	CREDIT

ANSWERS TO CHAPTER 7 EXERCISES (cont.)

Ex. 7 (cont.)

GENERAL JOURNAL PAGE ______

DATE 19 —		PARTICULARS	P.R.	DEBIT	CREDIT

 Name________________ Date____________

ANSWERS TO CHAPTER 7 EXERCISES (cont.)

Ex. 7 (cont.)

GENERAL JOURNAL

PAGE ________

DATE 19—		PARTICULARS	P.R.	DEBIT	CREDIT

 Name ____________ Date ____________

ANSWERS TO CHAPTER 7 EXERCISES (cont.)

Ex. 7 (cont.)

GENERAL JOURNAL

PAGE ______

DATE 19—		PARTICULARS	P.R.	DEBIT	CREDIT

 Name________________ Date________________

ANSWERS TO CHAPTER 7 EXERCISES (cont.)

Ex. 7 (cont.)

ACCOUNT Bank **NO.** 101

DATE 19 —		PARTICULARS	P.R.	DEBIT	CREDIT	DR CR	BALANCE

ACCOUNT Bank **NO.** 101

DATE 19 —		PARTICULARS	P.R.	DEBIT	CREDIT	DR CR	BALANCE

ANSWERS TO CHAPTER 7 EXERCISES (cont.)

Ex. 7 (cont.)

ACCOUNT Bank **NO.** 101

DATE 19 —		PARTICULARS	P.R.	DEBIT	CREDIT	DR CR	BALANCE

ACCOUNT A/R — L. Pero **NO.** 111

DATE 19 —		PARTICULARS	P.R.	DEBIT	CREDIT	DR CR	BALANCE

ACCOUNT A/R — K. Puna **NO.** 113

DATE 19 —		PARTICULARS	P.R.	DEBIT	CREDIT	DR CR	BALANCE

ACCOUNT A/R — Spectrum Co. **NO.** 115

DATE 19 —		PARTICULARS	P.R.	DEBIT	CREDIT	DR CR	BALANCE

ANSWERS TO CHAPTER 7 EXERCISES (cont.)

Ex. 7 (cont.)

ACCOUNT A/R — W.J. Thomson **NO.** 117

DATE 19 —		PARTICULARS	P.R.	DEBIT	CREDIT	DR CR	BALANCE

ACCOUNT Supplies **NO.** 120

DATE 19 —		PARTICULARS	P.R.	DEBIT	CREDIT	DR CR	BALANCE

ACCOUNT Equipment **NO.** 125

DATE 19 —		PARTICULARS	P.R.	DEBIT	CREDIT	DR CR	BALANCE

ACCOUNT Automobiles **NO.** 130

DATE 19 —		PARTICULARS	P.R.	DEBIT	CREDIT	DR CR	BALANCE

 Name ______________ Date ______________

ANSWERS TO CHAPTER 7 EXERCISES (cont.)

Ex. 7 (cont.)

ACCOUNT Bank Loan **NO.** 201

DATE 19 —		PARTICULARS	P.R.	DEBIT	CREDIT	DR CR	BALANCE

ACCOUNT A/P — Imperial Garage **NO.** 211

DATE 19 —		PARTICULARS	P.R.	DEBIT	CREDIT	DR CR	BALANCE

ACCOUNT A/P — Home Hardware **NO.** 213

DATE 19 —		PARTICULARS	P.R.	DEBIT	CREDIT	DR CR	BALANCE

ANSWERS TO CHAPTER 7 EXERCISES (cont.)

Ex. 7 (cont.)

ACCOUNT Sales Tax Payable **NO.** 220

DATE 19 —		PARTICULARS	P.R.	DEBIT	CREDIT	DR CR	BALANCE

ACCOUNT P. Schelling, Capital **NO.** 301

DATE 19 —		PARTICULARS	P.R.	DEBIT	CREDIT	DR CR	BALANCE

ACCOUNT P. Schelling, Drawings **NO.** 302

DATE 19 —		PARTICULARS	P.R.	DEBIT	CREDIT	DR CR	BALANCE

 Name______________ Date______________

ANSWERS TO CHAPTER 7 EXERCISES (cont.)

Ex. 7 (cont.)

ACCOUNT Service Revenue **NO.** 401

DATE 19—		PARTICULARS	P.R.	DEBIT	CREDIT	DR CR	BALANCE

ACCOUNT Automobiles Expense **NO.** 505

DATE 19—		PARTICULARS	P.R.	DEBIT	CREDIT	DR CR	BALANCE

ACCOUNT Bank Charges **NO.** 510

DATE 19—		PARTICULARS	P.R.	DEBIT	CREDIT	DR CR	BALANCE

 Name______________ Date__________

ANSWERS TO CHAPTER 7 EXERCISES (cont.)

Ex. 7 (cont.)

ACCOUNT General Expense **NO.** 515

DATE 19—		PARTICULARS	P.R.	DEBIT	CREDIT	DR CR	BALANCE

ACCOUNT Rent Expense **NO.** 520

DATE 19—		PARTICULARS	P.R.	DEBIT	CREDIT	DR CR	BALANCE

ACCOUNT Telephone Expense **NO.** 525

DATE 19—		PARTICULARS	P.R.	DEBIT	CREDIT	DR CR	BALANCE

ACCOUNT Wages Expense **NO.** 530

DATE 19—		PARTICULARS	P.R.	DEBIT	CREDIT	DR CR	BALANCE

ACCOUNT Loss on Sale of Equipment **NO.** 535

DATE 19—		PARTICULARS	P.R.	DEBIT	CREDIT	DR CR	BALANCE

 Name________________ Date____________

ANSWERS TO CHAPTER 7 EXERCISES (cont.)

Ex. 7 (cont.)

3. ______________________________

____

____

No.												

ANSWERS TO CHAPTER 7 EXERCISES (cont.)

Ex. 7 (cont.)

4. ______________________________

 Name______________________ Date________________

ANSWERS TO CHAPTER 7 EXERCISES (cont.)

Ex. 7 (cont.)

 Name________________ Date____________

ANSWERS TO CHAPTER 7 EXERCISES (cont.)

Exercise 8, p. 214

1. GENERAL JOURNAL PAGE ______

DATE 19 -7		PARTICULARS	P.R.	DEBIT	CREDIT

 Name________________ Date________________

ANSWERS TO CHAPTER 7 EXERCISES (cont.)

Ex. 8 (cont.)

GENERAL JOURNAL

PAGE ________

DATE 19-7		PARTICULARS	P.R.	DEBIT	CREDIT

 Name________________ Date________________

ANSWERS TO CHAPTER 7 EXERCISES (cont.)

Ex. 8 (cont.)

GENERAL JOURNAL

PAGE ______

DATE 19-7		PARTICULARS	P.R.	DEBIT	CREDIT

ANSWERS TO CHAPTER 7 EXERCISES (cont.)

Ex. 8 (cont.)

GENERAL JOURNAL PAGE ______

DATE 19-7		PARTICULARS	P.R.	DEBIT	CREDIT

 Name______________ Date______________

ANSWERS TO CHAPTER 7 EXERCISES (cont.)

Ex. 8 (cont.)

GENERAL JOURNAL

PAGE ______

DATE 19 -7		PARTICULARS	P.R.	DEBIT	CREDIT

ANSWERS TO CHAPTER 7 EXERCISES (cont.)

Ex. 8 (cont.)

ACCOUNT Bank **NO.** 100

DATE 19 -7		PARTICULARS	P.R.	DEBIT	CREDIT	DR CR	BALANCE
Sept.	30	Balance forwarded	—			D	3 750 20

ACCOUNT Bank **NO.** 100

DATE 19 -7		PARTICULARS	P.R.	DEBIT	CREDIT	DR CR	BALANCE

ACCOUNT Bank **NO.** 100

DATE 19 -7		PARTICULARS	P.R.	DEBIT	CREDIT	DR CR	BALANCE

ANSWERS TO CHAPTER 7 EXERCISES (cont.)

Ex. 8 (cont.)

ACCOUNT Bank **NO.** 100

DATE 19–7		PARTICULARS	P.R.	DEBIT	CREDIT	DR CR	BALANCE

ACCOUNT Supplies – Golf Course **NO.** 105

DATE 19–7		PARTICULARS	P.R.	DEBIT	CREDIT	DR CR	BALANCE
Sept.	30	Balance forwarded	—			D	10 236 –

ACCOUNT Supplies – Office **NO.** 110

DATE 19–7		PARTICULARS	P.R.	DEBIT	CREDIT	DR CR	BALANCE
Sept.	30	Balance forwarded	—			D	3 265 25

ACCOUNT Property **NO.** 115

DATE 19–7		PARTICULARS	P.R.	DEBIT	CREDIT	DR CR	BALANCE
Sept.	30	Balance forwarded	—			D	95 000 –

ACCOUNT Buildings **NO.** 120

DATE 19–7		PARTICULARS	P.R.	DEBIT	CREDIT	DR CR	BALANCE
Sept.	30	Balance forwarded	—			D	85 360 –

 Name________________ Date____________

ANSWERS TO CHAPTER 7 EXERCISES (cont.)

Ex. 8 (cont.)

ACCOUNT Automotive Equipment **NO.** 125

DATE 19 –7		PARTICULARS	P.R.	DEBIT	CREDIT	DR CR	BALANCE
Sept.	30	Balance forwarded	—			D	40 956 –

ACCOUNT Maintenance Equipment **NO.** 130

DATE 19 –7		PARTICULARS	P.R.	DEBIT	CREDIT	DR CR	BALANCE
Sept.	30	Balance forwarded	—			D	22 650 60

ACCOUNT Bank Loan **NO.** 200

DATE 19 –7		PARTICULARS	P.R.	DEBIT	CREDIT	DR CR	BALANCE
Sept.	30	Balance forwarded	—			C	120 000 –

ACCOUNT Accounts Payable – Main Supply **NO.** 205

DATE 19 –7		PARTICULARS	P.R.	DEBIT	CREDIT	DR CR	BALANCE
Sept.	30	Balance forwarded	—			C	1 890 65

 Name ____________ Date ____________

ANSWERS TO CHAPTER 7 EXERCISES (cont.)

Ex. 8 (cont.)

ACCOUNT Accounts Payable – Blair's Automotive **NO.** 210

DATE 19 –7		PARTICULARS	P.R.	DEBIT	CREDIT	DR CR	BALANCE

ACCOUNT Accounts Payable – Pro Equipment **NO.** 215

DATE 19 –7		PARTICULARS	P.R.	DEBIT	CREDIT	DR CR	BALANCE
Sept.	30	Balance forwarded	—			C	3 582 10

ACCOUNT Mortgage Payable **NO.** 220

DATE 19 –7		PARTICULARS	P.R.	DEBIT	CREDIT	DR CR	BALANCE
Sept.	30	Balance forwarded	—			C	100 000 –

ACCOUNT Shirley Iris, Capital **NO.** 300

DATE 19 –7		PARTICULARS	P.R.	DEBIT	CREDIT	DR CR	BALANCE
Sept.	30	Balance forwarded	—			C	37 802 96

ANSWERS TO CHAPTER 7 EXERCISES (cont.)

Ex. 8 (cont.)

ACCOUNT Shirley Iris, Drawings **NO.** 305

DATE 19 –7		PARTICULARS	P.R.	DEBIT	CREDIT	DR CR	BALANCE
Sept.	30	Balance forwarded	—			D	18 000 –

ACCOUNT Revenue – Golf **NO.** 400

DATE 19 –7		PARTICULARS	P.R.	DEBIT	CREDIT	DR CR	BALANCE
Sept.	30	Balance forwarded	—			C	52 655 –

ACCOUNT Revenue – Food **NO.** 405

DATE 19 –7		PARTICULARS	P.R.	DEBIT	CREDIT	DR CR	BALANCE
Sept.	30	Balance forwarded	—			C	9 250 50

ACCOUNT Automotive Expenses **NO.** 500

DATE 19 –7		PARTICULARS	P.R.	DEBIT	CREDIT	DR CR	BALANCE
Sept.	30	Balance forwarded	—			D	5 963 01

ANSWERS TO CHAPTER 7 EXERCISES (cont.)

Ex. 8 (cont.)

ACCOUNT Bank Charges **NO.** 505

DATE 19 –7		PARTICULARS	P.R.	DEBIT	CREDIT	DR CR	BALANCE
Sept.	30	Balance forwarded	—			D	6 842 25

ACCOUNT Light, Heat, and Water **NO.** 510

DATE 19 –7		PARTICULARS	P.R.	DEBIT	CREDIT	DR CR	BALANCE
Sept.	30	Balance forwarded	—			D	2 850 45

ACCOUNT Maintenance Expense **NO.** 515

DATE 19 –7		PARTICULARS	P.R.	DEBIT	CREDIT	DR CR	BALANCE
Sept.	30	Balance forwarded	—			D	7 230 85

ACCOUNT Miscellaneous Expense **NO.** 520

DATE 19 –7		PARTICULARS	P.R.	DEBIT	CREDIT	DR CR	BALANCE
Sept.	30	Balance forwarded	—			D	1 525 75

 Name________________________ Date________________

ANSWERS TO CHAPTER 7 EXERCISES (cont.)

Ex. 8 (cont.)

ACCOUNT Mortgage Interest **NO.** 525

DATE 19–7		PARTICULARS	P.R.	DEBIT	CREDIT	DR CR	BALANCE
Sept.	30	Balance forwarded	—			D	4 500 –

ACCOUNT Telephone Expense **NO.** 530

DATE 19–7		PARTICULARS	P.R.	DEBIT	CREDIT	DR CR	BALANCE
Sept.	30	Balance forwarded	—			D	685 55

ACCOUNT Wages Expense **NO.** 535

DATE 19–7		PARTICULARS	P.R.	DEBIT	CREDIT	DR CR	BALANCE
Sept.	30	Balance forwarded	—			D	16 365 30

 Name____________________ Date________________

ANSWERS TO CHAPTER 7 EXERCISES (cont.)

Ex. 8 (cont.)

2.

 Name________________ Date________________

ANSWERS TO CHAPTER 7 EXERCISES (cont.)

Ex. 8 (cont.)

3.

ANSWERS TO CHAPTER 7 EXERCISES (cont.)

Ex. 8 (cont.)

4.

 Name________________ Date________________

ANSWERS TO CHAPTER 7 EXERCISES (cont.)

FOR FURTHER THOUGHT

Exercise 9, p. 217

1. ______________________________

2. ______________________________

3. ______________________________

4. ______________________________

5. ______________________________

6. ______________________________

7. ______________________________

8. ______________________________

9. ______________________________

10. ______________________________

Chapter 7

Name ______________________ Date ______________

CASE STUDIES (text, p. 217)

Case 1 *"To Fire or Not To Fire,"* p. 217

1. ______________________

2. ______________________

3. ______________________

4. ______________________

5. ______________________

 Name________________ Date________________

CASE STUDIES (cont.)

Case 2 *Frustration for the Auditor*, p. 218

1.

GENERAL JOURNAL PAGE ________

DATE 19—		PARTICULARS	P.R.	DEBIT	CREDIT

 Name________________ Date__________

CASE STUDIES (cont.)

Case 2 (cont.)

GENERAL JOURNAL

PAGE ______

DATE 19—		PARTICULARS	P.R.	DEBIT	CREDIT

 Name __________ Date __________

CASE STUDIES (cont.)

Case 2 (cont.)

2.

Case 3 *Is Bank Accounting Different?*, p. 219

Case 4 *Does Automated Accounting Use Standard Theory?*, p. 219

1.

2.

ENTREPRENEUR Leslie Hayes/Electraslide Corporation

ANSWERS TO DISCUSSION QUESTIONS (text, p. 221)

1.

2.

3.

4.

5.

 Name__________ Date__________

Chapter 8 The Work Sheet and Formal Financial Statements

ANSWERS TO SECTION 8.1 REVIEW QUESTIONS (text, p. 230)

The Six-Column Work Sheet

1. __________

2. __________

3. __________

4. __________

5. __________

6. __________

7. __________

8. __________

9. __________

10. __________

11. __________

12. __________

13. __________

14. 1) __________
    2) __________
    3) __________
    4) __________
    5) __________
    6) __________

Chapter 8

Name_______________ Date_______________

ANSWERS TO SECTION 8.1 EXERCISES (text, p. 231)

Exercise 1, p. 231

Indicate to which column in the worksheet each account should be extended by placing a check in the appropriate column.

Account	Income Statement Debit	Income Statement Credit	Balance Sheet Debit	Balance Sheet Credit
Accounts Payable				
Miscellaneous Expense				
Revenue				
Advertising Expense				
Wages Expense				
Mortgage Payable				
Light and Heat Expense				
Equipment				
G. Rojek, Capital				
Delivery Expense				
Bank Loan				
Accounts Receivable				
Automobile				
Bank				
G. Rojek, Drawings				
Sales				
Bank Charges Expense				
Rent Expense				
Supplies				
Trucks				

 Name____________________ Date________________

ANSWERS TO SECTION 8.1 EXERCISES (cont.)

Exercise 2, p. 231

ACCOUNTS	TRIAL BALANCE		INCOME STATEMENT		BALANCE SHEET	
	DR.	CR.	DR.	CR.	DR.	CR.

ANSWERS TO SECTION 8.1 EXERCISES (cont.)

Exercise 3, p. 232 (Workbook Exercise)

From the simplified data shown below, complete a work sheet for Crest Consulting for the year ended December 31, 19 —. (Loss situation.)

TRIAL BALANCE DECEMBER 31, 19 —

Bank	$ 3 050.91	
Accounts Receivable	46 295.10	
Supplies	3 165.00	
Equipment	10 515.00	
Automobiles	50 900.00	
Bank Loan		$ 40 000.00
Accounts Payable		8 887.98
A. Fox, Capital		100 000.00
A. Fox, Drawings	20 746.00	
Commissions Earned		116 500.00
Bank Charges Expense	6 421.12	
Car Expense	18 374.50	
Miscellaneous Expense	1 857.00	
Light and Heat Expense	12 016.20	
Rent Expense	24 000.00	
Telephone Expense	3 675.00	
Wages Expense	64 372.15	
	$ 265 387.98	$ 265 387.98

ANSWERS TO SECTION 8.1 EXERCISES (cont.)

Ex. 3 (cont.)

ACCOUNTS	TRIAL BALANCE		INCOME STATEMENT		BALANCE SHEET	
	DR.	CR.	DR.	CR.	DR.	CR.

Chapter 8

Name________________________ Date____________________

ANSWERS TO SECTION 8.1 EXERCISES (cont.)

Exercise 4, p. 232

ACCOUNTS	TRIAL BALANCE		INCOME STATEMENT		BALANCE SHEET	
	DR.	CR.	DR.	CR.	DR.	CR.

Chapter 8

Name ______________________ Date ______________

ANSWERS TO SECTION 8.1 EXERCISES (cont.)

Exercise 5, p. 232

1.

Work Sheet — *The Arthur Company* — *Month Ended Oct. 31, 19 —*

ACCOUNTS	TRIAL BALANCE DR	TRIAL BALANCE CR	INCOME STATEMENT DR	INCOME STATEMENT CR	BALANCE SHEET DR	BALANCE SHEET CR
Bank	1 722.16				1 722.16	
Acc. Rec'l — J. Young	323.—				332.—	
Acc. Rec'l — M. Watson	72.—				72.—	
Acc. Rec'l — H. Chan	116.—				116.—	
Supplies	1 255.—				1 255.—	
Office Equipment	5 863.—				5 863.—	
Automobiles	13 200.—				1 320.—	
Acc. Pay'l — O.K. Supply		421.72				421.72
Acc. Pay'l — City Hydro		116.42				116.42
Acc. Pay'l — Slick Oil Co.		331.19				331.19
Bank Loan		10 000.—				10 000.—
P. Arthur, Capital		10 504.82				10 504.82
P. Arthur, Drawings	1 000.—			1 000.—		
Revenue		4 903.17		4 903.17		
Advertising	465.12		465.12			
Automobile Expense	270.—				270.—	
Bank Charges	56.40		56.40			
Miscellaneous Exp.	113.74		113.74			
Rent	400.—		400.—			
Salaries	1 280.—		1 280.—		1 280	
Telephone	25.60		25.60			
Utilities	115.30					
	26 277.32	26 277.32	2 340.86	5 903.17	12 230.16	21 074.15
Net Income			3 562.31			8 843.99
			5 903.17	5 903.17	12 230.16	29 918.14

 Name________________ Date________________

ANSWERS TO SECTION 8.1 EXERCISES (cont.)

Ex. 5 (cont.)

2. Accounts Receivable Control ________
Accounts Payable Control ________

ANSWERS TO SECTION 8.1 EXERCISES (cont.)

Exercise 6, p. 232

Show where each step in the accounting cycle should appear in the chart to the right by entering the number of its location in the circle provided.

STEPS IN THE ACCOUNTING CYCLE

WORK SHEET PREPARED ◯

LEDGER BALANCED BY MEANS OF A TRIAL BALANCE ◯

TRANSACTIONS OCCUR SOURCE DOCUMENTS ◯

PERFORMED BY SENIOR PERSONNEL ◯

ACCOUNTING ENTRIES RECORDED IN THE JOURNAL ◯

BALANCE SHEET AND INCOME STATEMENT PREPARED ◯

PERFORMED BY JUNIOR PERSONNEL ◯

JOURNAL ENTRIES POSTED TO THE LEDGER ACCOUNTS ◯

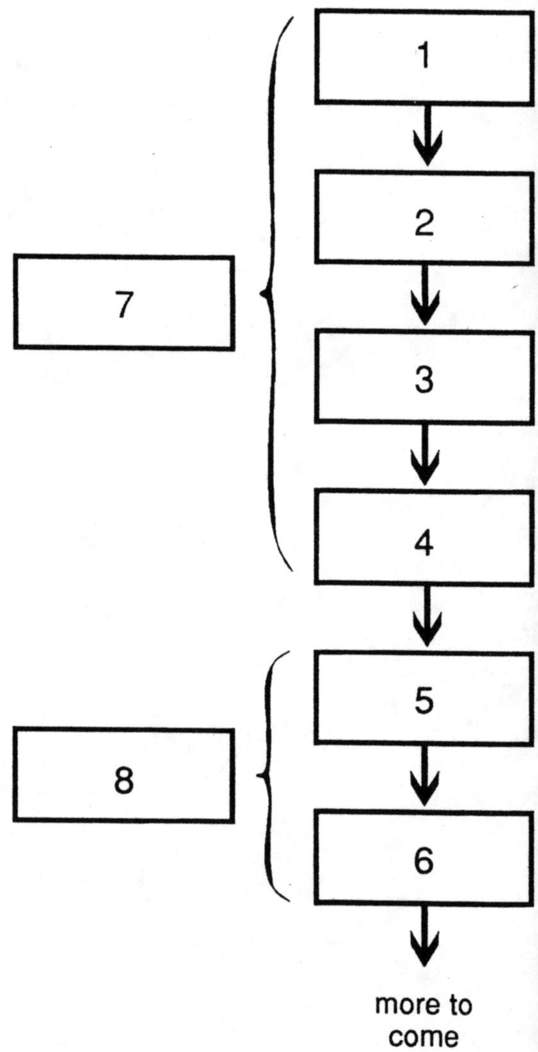

Chapter 8

Name____________________ Date________________

ANSWERS TO SECTION 8.2 REVIEW QUESTIONS (text, p. 235)

Formal Financial Statements: Income Statement

1. ____

2. ____

3. ____

4. ____

5. ____

6. ____

7. ____

Name ______________________ Date ________________

ANSWERS TO SECTION 8.2 EXERCISES (text, p. 236)

Exercise 1, p. 236

1. ____________________

2. ____________________

3. ____________________

4. ____________________

5. ____________________

 Name ______________ Date ______________

ANSWERS TO SECTION 8.2 EXERCISES (cont.)

Exercise 2, p. 236

 Name________________________ Date________________

ANSWERS TO SECTION 8.2 EXERCISES (cont.)

Exercise 3, p. 237

1. ____

____

____

____

____

____

____

____

2. The correct figure for the Net Income is__________.

Chapter 8

Name ____________________ Date ____________________

ANSWERS TO SECTION 8.3 REVIEW QUESTIONS (text, p. 243)

Formal Financial Statements: Balance Sheet

1. ______________________________
2. ______________________________
3. ______________________________
4. ______________________________
5. ______________________________
6. ______________________________
7. ______________________________
8. ______________________________
____
____
9. ______________________________
____
10. 1) ________ 2) ________ 3) ________________
11. ______________________________
12. 1) ______________________________
2) ______________________________
13. ______________________________

Chapter 8

Name ______________________ Date ________________

ANSWERS TO SECTION 8.3 EXERCISES (text, p. 244)

Exercise 1, p. 244

ACCOUNTS	CLASSIFICATION
Accounts Payable	______________
Accounts Receivable	______________
Advertising Expense	______________
Automobiles	______________
Bank Charges Expense	______________
Bank Loan	______________
Bank	______________
Buildings	______________
Commissions Earned	______________
Delivery Expense	______________
F. Ryback, Capital	______________
F. Ryback, Drawings	______________
General Expense	______________
Insurance Expense	______________
Mortgage Payable (Current Instalment)	______________
Mortgage Payable (Non-current portion)	______________
Postage	______________
Rent	______________
Supplies	______________
Telephone	______________
Wages Expense	______________

Exercise 2, p. 244

1. Current assets: ____________
2. Fixed assets: ____________
3. Current liabilities: ____________
4. Long-term liabilities: ____________
5. ____
6. ____
7. Mortgage payable: ____________

Chapter 8

Name________________________ Date__________________

ANSWERS TO SECTION 8.3 EXERCISES (cont.)

Exercise 3, p. 245

Complete the following schedule by filling in the blanks.

Items	*Opening Capital*	*Net Income or Net Loss (–)*	*Drawings*	*Ending Capital*
a.	$ 30 000	$ 15 000	$ 10 000	$
b.	50 000	–2 000	7 000	
c.	70 000	32 000		75 500
d.		16 000	19 500	33 200
e.	56 000		30 000	40 000
f.	45 000		25 000	15 000
g.	22 000		10 000	28 000
h.		25 000	18 000	42 000
i.	120 000	42 000		112 000

Exercise 4, p. 246

 Name________________ Date__________

ANSWERS TO SECTION 8.3 EXERCISES (cont.)

Ex. 4 (cont.)

ANSWERS TO SECTION 8.3 EXERCISES (cont.)

Exercise 5, p. 246

Name____________________ Date________________

ANSWERS TO SECTION 8.3 EXERCISES (cont.)

Exercise 6, p. 247

Chapter 8

Name________________________ Date____________________

ANSWERS TO CHAPTER 8 EXERCISES (text, p. 248)

USING YOUR KNOWLEDGE

Exercise 1, p. 248

1. ____

____

2. ____

____

____

 Name______________________ Date__________________

ANSWERS TO CHAPTER 8 EXERCISES (cont.)

Exercise 2, p. 249

ACCOUNTS	TRIAL BALANCE		INCOME STATEMENT		BALANCE SHEET	
	DR.	CR.	DR.	CR.	DR.	CR.

 Name________________ Date____________

ANSWERS TO CHAPTER 8 EXERCISES (cont.)

Ex. 2 (cont.)

2.

 Name________________ Date____________

ANSWERS TO CHAPTER 8 EXERCISES (cont.)

Ex. 2 (cont.)

3. ____

 Name________________________ Date__________________

ANSWERS TO CHAPTER 8 EXERCISES (cont.)

Exercise 3, p. 249

ACCOUNTS	TRIAL BALANCE		INCOME STATEMENT		BALANCE SHEET	
	DR.	CR.	DR.	CR.	DR.	CR.

 Name________________ Date________________

ANSWERS TO CHAPTER 8 EXERCISES (cont.)

Ex. 3 (cont.)

 Name________________ Date________________

ANSWERS TO CHAPTER 8 EXERCISES (cont.)

Ex. 3 (cont.)

 Name ______________ Date ______________

ANSWERS TO CHAPTER 8 EXERCISES (cont.)

Exercise 4, p. 250

ACCOUNTS	TRIAL BALANCE		INCOME STATEMENT		BALANCE SHEET	
	DR.	CR.	DR.	CR.	DR.	CR.

 Name________________ Date________________

ANSWERS TO CHAPTER 8 EXERCISES (cont.)

Ex. 4 (cont.)

 Name____________________ Date______________

ANSWERS TO CHAPTER 8 EXERCISES (cont.)

Ex. 4 (cont.)

ANSWERS TO CHAPTER 8 EXERCISES (cont.)

Exercise 5, p. 250

For each of the following, check off the most appropriate response in the space provided.

1. Financial statements are prepared
   a. once a year. ☐
   b. at the end of the fiscal period. ☐
   c. whenever management requires it. ☐
   d. all of the above. ☐
   e. none of the above. ☐

2. A work sheet is
   a. one of the books of account. ☐
   b. one of the financial statements. ☐
   c. used instead of the financial statements. ☐
   d. all of the above. ☐
   e. none of the above. ☐

3. Extending amounts on a work sheet means
   a. adding to the amounts because of additional transactions. ☐
   b. placing debit amounts in debit columns and credit amounts in credit columns. ☐
   c. transferring amounts into the Balance Sheet section or the Income Statement section. ☐
   d. all of the above. ☐
   e. none of the above. ☐

4. The process of balancing the work sheet involves
   a. totaling the four right-hand money columns. ☐
   b. calculating the difference between the two money columns in each of the last two sections. ☐
   c. ensuring that the differences in b) above are equal to each other. ☐

ANSWERS TO CHAPTER 8 EXERCISES (cont.)

Ex. 5 (cont.)

d. all of the above. ☐

e. none of the above. ☐

5. A work sheet will not balance if

a. the Telephone Expense amount is extended to the Balance Sheet section Debit Column. ☐

b. the Drawings amount is extended to the Income Statement section Debit column. ☐

c. the Capital amount is extended to the Balance Sheet section Debit column. ☐

d. all of the above. ☐

e. none of the above. ☐

6. You can tell what the net income figure is by

a. looking at the balancing figure in the Balance Sheet section of the work sheet. ☐

b. looking at the balancing figure in the Income Statement section of the work sheet. ☐

c. looking at the equity section of the completed balance sheet. ☐

d. all of the above. ☐

e. none of the above. ☐

7. All of the following statements, except one, are false. Indicate the one which is true.

a. The report form of balance sheet is the only style used in the real business world. ☐

b. The report form of balance sheet is common because it uses standard-sized paper. ☐

c. The report form of balance sheet is horizontal in form. ☐

d. The style of the report form of balance sheet eliminates the need for "balancing" totals. ☐

e. The report form of balance sheet is more difficult to understand. ☐

ANSWERS TO CHAPTER 8 EXERCISES (cont.)

Ex. 5 (cont.)

8. All of the following statements, except one, are false. Indicate the one that is true.

On a classified balance sheet:

a. Automobiles are not included in the Fixed Assets section because their value decreases over time. ☐

b. A mortgage payable is deducted from the asset Building. ☐

c. Supplies are not included as a current asset because they are not normally converted into cash. ☐

d. A bank loan is included in long-term liabilities. ☐

e. The values shown for the fixed assets are not necessarily their true market value. ☐

9. All of the following statements, except one, are true. Indicate the one that is false.

a. The data in the books of account are considered to be "raw" data. ☐

b. Accountants are judged on the basis of the accounting statements and reports that they prepare. Therefore, their work should be first-class in form and content. ☐

c. All of the data necessary for the financial statements can be found on the work sheet. ☐

d. An overall decrease in capital can occur in two ways. An overall increase in capital can occur in only one way. Therefore, decreases in capital are more common. ☐

e. The beginning balance in the equity section of the balance sheet is not always that of January 1. ☐

10. During a fiscal period a business suffered a loss of $12 000, began the period with a capital balance of $20 000, and ended the period with a minus capital balance of $2 000. The drawings for the fiscal period were:

a. $6 000. ☐

b. $10 000. ☐

c. $30 000. ☐

d. $18 000. ☐

e. $14 000. ☐

 Name ____________ Date ____________

ANSWERS TO CHAPTER 8 EXERCISES (cont.)

FOR FURTHER THOUGHT

Exercise 6, p. 252

1. ____________

2. ____________

3. ____________

1) ____________
2) ____________
3) ____________

4. ____________

5. ____________

6. ____________

7. ____________

8. ____________

1) ____________
2) ____________
3) ____________
4) ____________
5) ____________

9. ____________

10. ____________

Chapter 8

Name ______________________ Date ______________

CASE STUDIES (text, p. 253)

Case 1 *Interpreting Balance Sheets*, p. 253

1. ____________________

2. ____________________

3. ____________________

4. ____________________

Case 2 *Financing Student Council Activities*, p. 253

1. ____________________

2. ____________________

CASE STUDIES (cont.)

Case 2 (cont.)

3. ____________

4. ____________

Case 3 *Responsibility for Loss?*, p. 254

1. a) ____________
b) (i) ____________
(ii) ____________
(iii) ____________
c) ____________

2. a) ____________
b) ____________
c) ____________

Case 4 *Solving a Money Problem, p. 255*

1. ____________

2. ____________

3. ____________

4. a) ____________
b) ____________
c) i) ____________
ii) ____________
d) ____________

CASE STUDIES (cont.)

Case 4 (cont.)

5.

Chapter 8

Name______________________ Date______________

CAREER Carol Smalley/Accounts Payable Supervisor

ANSWERS TO DISCUSSION QUESTIONS (text, p. 258)

1.

2.

3.

4.

5.

6.

7.

Chapter 9 Completing the Accounting Cycle

ANSWERS TO SECTION 9.1 REVIEW QUESTIONS (text, p. 272)

Simple Adjustments and Expanded Work Sheets

1. ______________________________

2. ______________________________

3. ______________________________

4. ______________________________

5. ______________________________

6. ______________________________

7. ______________________________

8. ______________________________

9. ______________________________

10. ______________________________

11. ______________________________

12. ______________________________

13. ______________________________

14. ______________________________

15. ______________________________

16. ______________________________

Chapter 9

Name________________________ Date________________

ANSWERS TO SECTION 9.1 EXERCISES (text, p. 272)

Exercise 1, p. 272

Complete the following schedule.

Supplies	*Trial Balance Figure*	*Supplies Closing Inventory Figure*	*Supplies Expense Figure*
1.	$300.00	$100.00	
2.		$175.00	$250.00
3.	$950.00		$740.00
Prepaid Insurance	*Trial Balance Figure*	*Prepaid Insurance Final Calculation*	*Insurance Expense Figure*
1.	$875.00	$325.00	
2.	$925		$315.00
3.		$410.00	$375.00

Exercise 2, p. 272

Using the following information, complete the inventory sheet and make the adjusting entry in the T-accounts.

Inventory Listing

Inventory Item	Quantity		Unit Price		Value	
Rubber bands	3	boxes	$ 1.50	per box		
Envelopes #8	10	boxes	32.00	per box		
Envelopes # 10	4 1/2	boxes	36.00	per box		
Envelopes, manila	2	boxes	28.00	per box		
Typing paper	4M	sheets	15.60	per M		
Letterhead	10M	sheets	22.50	per M		
Copy paper	4M	sheets	10.00	per M		
Carbon paper	2	boxes	6.00	per box		
Paper clips	12	boxes	1.50	per box		
Staples	15	boxes	4.10	per box		
Pencils, regular	4	doz	5.50	per doz		
Pencils, red	2	doz	6.10	per doz		
				Total		

Supplies	
2 018.–	

Supplies Used	

 Name________________ Date________________

ANSWERS TO SECTION 9.1 EXERCISES (cont.)

Exercise 3, p. 273

Year	*Insurance Expense*	*Prepaid Insurance (Dec. 31)*
19–1		
19–2		
	Total Expense $216	

Exercise 4, p. 273

	Total number of months of insurance used as of the designated year-end	*Total number of months of insurance unused as of the designated year-end*	*Value of the prepaid insurance at the designated year-end*
a.			
b.			
c.			
d.			
e.			
f.			

Exercise 5, p. 274

1. ________________
____
2. ________________
3. ________________
4. ________________
____
5. ________________
6. ________________
7. ________________

 Name ________________ Date ________________

ANSWERS TO SECTION 9.1 EXERCISES (cont.)

Ex. 6, p. 274

1.

Work Sheet — **P. Pahl and Company** — **Year Ended December 31, 19–8**

ACCOUNTS	TRIAL BALANCE		ADJUSTMENTS		ADJUSTED T. B.		INCOME STATEMENT		BALANCE SHEET	
	DEBIT	CREDIT	DEBIT	CREDIT	DEBIT	CREDIT	DEBIT	CREDIT	DEBIT	CREDIT
Bank	1 800									
Accounts Receivable	19 500									
Supplies	1 000									
Ppd. Insurance	1 750									
Equipment	22 000									
Automobile	21 000									
Accounts Payable		4 360								
P. Pahl, Capital		54 040								
P. Pahl, Drawings	15 000									
Fees Earned		60 300								
Car Expense	3 800									
General Expense	2 950									
Miscellaneous Exp.	700									
Rent Expense	7 200									
Wages Expense	22 000									
	118 700	118 700								

ANSWERS TO SECTION 9.1 EXERCISES (cont.)

Ex. 6 (cont.)

2. GENERAL JOURNAL PAGE ______

DATE 19–8		PARTICULARS	P.R.	DEBIT	CREDIT

3.

Account	Debit	Credit
Bank	1 800	
Accounts Payable		4 360
P. Pahl, Capital		54 040
Accounts Receivable	19 500	
P. Pahl, Drawings	15 000	
Supplies	1 000	
Fees Earned		60 300
Prepaid Insurance	1 750	
Car Expense	3 800	

ANSWERS TO SECTION 9.1 EXERCISES (cont.)

Ex. 6 (cont.)

3. (cont.)

Equipment	
22 000	

Automobile	
21 000	

General Expense	
2 950	

Miscellaneous Expense	
700	

Rent Expense	
7 200	

Wages Expense	
22 000	

Supplies Expense	

Insurance Expense	

 Name________________ Date________________

ANSWERS TO SECTION 9.1 EXERCISES (cont.)

Ex. 6 (cont.)

Optional

4.

ANSWERS TO SECTION 9.1 EXERCISES (cont.)

Ex. 6 (cont.)

4. (cont.)

Name ____________ Date ____________

ANSWERS TO SECTION 9.1 EXERCISES (cont.)

Ex. 7, p. 275

1.

Work Sheet **Mission Marketing** **Year Ended December 31, 19–5**

ACCOUNTS	TRIAL BALANCE		ADJUSTMENTS		ADJUSTED T. B.		INCOME STATEMENT		BALANCE SHEET	
	DEBIT	CREDIT	DEBIT	CREDIT	DEBIT	CREDIT	DEBIT	CREDIT	DEBIT	CREDIT
Bank	3 000									
Accounts Receivable	21 600									
Supplies	4 250									
Ppd. Insurance	1 254									
Equipment	19 200									
Automobile	44 200									
Accounts Payable		7 345								
C. Ans, Capital		71 275								
C. Ans, Drawings	40 000									
Fees Earned		135 700								
Car Expense	13 214									
Light and Power Exp.	2 800									
Miscellaneous Exp.	1 563									
Rent Expense	18 000									
Wages Expense	45 239									
	214 320	214 320								

 Name________________ Date________________

ANSWERS TO SECTION 9.1 EXERCISES (cont.)

Ex. 7 (cont.)

2.

GENERAL JOURNAL

PAGE ________

DATE 19—5		PARTICULARS	P.R.	DEBIT	CREDIT

3.

Bank	
3 000	

Accounts Payable	
	7 345

C. Ans, Capital	
	71 275

Accounts Receivable	
21 600	

C. Ans, Drawings	
40 000	

Supplies	
4 250	

Fees Earned	
	135 700

Prepaid Insurance	
1 254	

Car Expense	
13 214	

ANSWERS TO SECTION 9.1 EXERCISES (cont.)

Ex. 7 (cont.)

3. (cont.)

Equipment	
19 200	

Automobile	
44 200	

Light and Power Expense	
2 800	

Miscellaneous Expense	
1 563	

Rent Expense	
18 000	

Wages Expense	
45 239	

Supplies Expense	

Insurance Expense	

ANSWERS TO SECTION 9.1 EXERCISES (cont.)

Ex. 7 (cont.)

Optional

4.

____

____

____

ANSWERS TO SECTION 9.1 EXERCISES (cont.)

Ex. 7 (cont.)

4. (cont.)

ANSWERS TO SECTION 9.1 EXERCISES (cont.)

Ex. 8, p. 276

1.

J. Soo and Associates

Work Sheet

Year Ended December 31, 19–5

ACCOUNTS	TRIAL BALANCE		ADJUSTMENTS		INCOME STATEMENT		BALANCE SHEET	
	DEBIT	CREDIT	DEBIT	CREDIT	DEBIT	CREDIT	DEBIT	CREDIT
Bank	2 500							
Accounts Receivable	11 500							
Supplies	1 950							
Ppd. Insurance	624							
Equipment	9 200							
Automobile	18 350							
Accounts Payable		6 230						
P. Pahl, Capital		36 662						
P. Pahl, Drawings	7 500							
Commissions		35 650						
Car Expense	3 214							
Light and Power Exp.	1 563							
Miscellaneous Exp.	902							
Rent Expense	6 000							
Wages Expense	15 239							
	78 542	78 542						

ANSWERS TO SECTION 9.1 EXERCISES (cont.)

Ex. 8 (cont.)

2. GENERAL JOURNAL PAGE ______

DATE 19—		PARTICULARS	P.R.	DEBIT	CREDIT

3.

Account	Debit	Credit
Bank	2 500	
Accounts Payable		6 230
J. Soo, Capital		36 662
Accounts Receivable	11 500	
J. Soo, Drawings	7 500	
Supplies	1 950	
Commissions		35 650
Prepaid Insurance	624	
Car Expense	3 214	
Equipment	9 200	
General Expense	1 563	
Automobiles	18 350	
Miscellaneous Expense	902	

 Name________________ Date________________

ANSWERS TO SECTION 9.1 EXERCISES (cont.)

Ex. 8 (cont.)

3. (cont.)

Rent Expense	
6 000	

Wages Expense	
15 239	

Supplies Expense	

Insurance Expense	

ANSWERS TO SECTION 9.1 EXERCISES (cont.)

Ex. 8 (cont.)

Optional

4.

 Name________________________ Date________________

ANSWERS TO SECTION 9.1 EXERCISES (cont.)

Ex. 8 (cont.)

4. (cont.)

 Name ______________ Date ______________

ANSWERS TO SECTION 9.2 REVIEW QUESTIONS (text, p. 279)

Closing Entries Concepts

1. ______________

2. ______________

3. ______________

4. ______________

5. ______________

6. ______________

7. ______________

8. ______________

9. ______________
   1) ______________
   2) ______________
   3) ______________

10. ______________

ANSWERS TO SECTION 9.2 EXERCISES (text, p. 280)

Exercise 1, p. 280

ANSWERS TO SECTION 9.2 EXERCISES (cont.)

Exercise 2, p. 280

1., 2.

Account	Debit	Credit
Bank	100	
Bank Loan		300
S. Mosar, Capital		740
S. Mosar, Drawings	750	
Accounts Receivable	200	
Accounts Payable		150
Advertising Revenue		1 750
Sales Revenue		450
Supplies	50	
Bank Charges	20	
Light and Heat	40	
Equipment	1 050	
Miscellaneous Exp.	5	
Printing Expense	500	
Rent	250	
Telephone	25	
Wages	400	

ANSWERS TO SECTION 9.2 EXERCISES (cont.)

Exercise 2 (cont.)

1., 2. (cont.)

 Name__________________ Date______________

ANSWERS TO SECTION 9.2 EXERCISES (cont.)

Exercise 3, p. 280 (Workbook Exercise)

In the chart below, the steps in the accounting cycle are given in incorrect order.

Required: 1. In the column headed Step No. enter the correct step number according to the sequence of steps given in the text.

2. In two of the remaining five columns place check marks to indicate when the step is performed and by whom.

STEPS IN THE ACCOUNTING CYCLE	STEP NO.	DONE DAILY	DONE MONTHLY	DONE AT THE END OF THE FISCAL PERIOD	DONE BY JUNIOR PERSONNEL	DONE BY SENIOR PERSONNEL
Journal entries posted to the ledger accounts.						
Adjusting and closing entries journalized and posted.						
Post-closing trial balance.						
Financial statements prepared.						
Ledger balanced by means of a trial balance.						
Accounting entries recorded in the journal.						
Work sheet prepared.						
Transactions occur.						

Exercise 4, p. 280

1. Accounting is ________ in nature.
2. The ____________________ states that financial reporting is done in equal periods of time.
3. Asset and liability accounts are considered to be ____ accounts.
4. ______________ are ones that have their balances continue on into the succeeding fiscal period.
5. Revenue, expense, and drawings accounts are considered to be ________ accounts.
6. The balances in ________________ do not continue into the ____ fiscal period.

 Name________________ Date________________

ANSWERS TO SECTION 9.2 EXERCISES (cont.)

Ex. 4 (cont.)

7. Another name for nominal account is a ________________
8. Nominal accounts begin each fiscal period with ________________
9. The process of removing the "old" balances from the nominal accounts is known as ________________ ________________
10. ________________ means to cause it to have no balance.
11. During a fiscal period the Capital account shows ________________
12. Changes in equity during a fiscal period (except for additional investments by the owner) are contained in ________________ accounts.
13. At the end of the fiscal period the ledger is brought up to date by ________________ ________________
14. One of the final steps in the accounting cycle is to bring the Capital account ________ and to ________ the nominal accounts.
15. The final step in the accounting cycle is ________________

List of Words and Phrases

a nil balance	nominal accounts
close out	real
closing an account	real accounts
closing the accounts	revenue, expense, and drawings
cyclical	temporary equity account
next	the balance at the beginning of the period
journalizing and posting the adjusting entries	the post-closing trial balance
	Time Period Concept
nominal	up to date

 Name________________________ Date________________

ANSWERS TO SECTION 9.3 REVIEW QUESTIONS (text, p. 288)

Journalizing and Posting the Closing Entries

1. ____________________
2. ____________________
3. ____________________
4. ____________________
5. ____________________
6. ____________________
7. ____________________
8. ____________________
   1) ____________________
   2) ____________________
   3) ____________________
   4) ____________________

Chapter 9

Name ______________________ Date ______________

ANSWERS TO SECTION 9.3 EXERCISES (text, p. 288)

Exercise 1, p. 288

GENERAL JOURNAL PAGE ________

DATE		PARTICULARS	P.R.	DEBIT	CREDIT

 Name________________ Date________________

ANSWERS TO SECTION 9.3 EXERCISES (cont.)

Exercise 2, p. 289

1. **GENERAL JOURNAL** PAGE ______

DATE		PARTICULARS	P.R.	DEBIT	CREDIT

ANSWERS TO SECTION 9.3 EXERCISES (cont.)

Ex. 2 (cont.)

2. **General Ledger for Golden Tresses Hair Stylists**

Bank	
790	

Supplies, Materials	
2 755	

Prepaid Insurance	
2 450	

Equipment	
17 370	

Accounts Payable	
	1 075

R. Tompko, Capital	
	9 922

R. Tompko, Drawings	
42 000	

Revenue	
	98 370

Advertising Expense	
1 200	

Bank Charges Expense	
96	

Light and Heat Expense	
2 104	

Materials Used Expense	
6 950	

Miscellaneous Expense	
1 902	

Rent Expense	
6 000	

Wages Expense	
25 750	

Insurance Expense	

Income Summary	

 Name________________ Date____________

ANSWERS TO SECTION 9.3 EXERCISES (cont.)

Ex. 2 (cont.)

3.

____

____

____

			DR	CR

Exercise 3, p. 289 (Workbook Exercise)

Shown below is the completed work sheet for Richard Koehler who operates a dance hall in Moose Jaw, Saskatchewan.

1. Journalize the adjusting and closing entries in the general journal provided.
2. Post the adjusting and closing entries in the general ledger provided.
3. Take off a post-closing trial balance.

Ex. 3 (cont.)

Richard Koehler — Work Sheet — Year Ended December 31, 19—

ACCOUNTS	TRIAL BALANCE DR	TRIAL BALANCE CR	ADJUSTMENTS DR	ADJUSTMENTS CR	INCOME STATEMENT DR	INCOME STATEMENT CR	BALANCE SHEET DR	BALANCE SHEET CR
Bank	1 057 60						1 057 60	
Accounts Receivable	9 357 —						9 357 —	
Supplies	3 746 —			1 702 —			2 044 —	
Prepaid Insurance	3 750 —			2 430 —			1 320 —	
Tapes & Records	8 747 —			2 537 —			6 210 —	
Sound Equipment	18 800 26						18 800 26	
Truck	9 065 —						9 065 —	
Accounts Payable		2 016 50		185 —				2 201 50
Bank Loan		5 000 —						5 000 —
R. Koehler, Capital		57 773 77						57 773 77
R. Koehler, Drawings	10 000 —						10 000 —	
Revenue – Admissions		41 375 —				41 375 —		
Revenue – Concessions		15 960 —				15 960 —		
Advertising Expense	2 740 —				2 740 —			
Bank Charges Expense	742 —				742 —			
Concession Costs Expense	15 376 10		110 —		15 486 10			
Light & Heat Expense	3 431 01				3 431 01			
Miscellaneous Expense	547 30		75 —		622 30			
Musicians' Fees Expense	4 316 —				4 316 —			
Rent Expense	12 000 —				12 000 —			

(CONTINUED NEXT PAGE)

Name ______________________ Date ________________

Ex. 3 (cont.)

Richard Koehler — Work Sheet — Year Ended December 31, 19—

ACCOUNTS	TRIAL BALANCE DR	TRIAL BALANCE CR	ADJUSTMENTS DR	ADJUSTMENTS CR	INCOME STATEMENT DR	INCOME STATEMENT CR	BALANCE SHEET DR	BALANCE SHEET CR
Wages	18 450 —				18 450 —			
	122 125 27	122 125 27						
Supplies Expense			1 702 —		1 702 —			
Insurance Expense			2 430 —		2 430 —			
Tapes & Records Exp.			2 537 —		2 537 —			
			6 854 —	6 854 —	64 456 41	57 335 —	57 853 86	64 975 27
						7 121 41	7 121 41	
Net Loss					64 456 41	64 456 41	64 975 27	64 975 27

 Name ______________ Date ______________

ANSWERS TO SECTION 9.3 EXERCISES (cont.)

Ex. 3 (cont.)

GENERAL JOURNAL

PAGE ______

DATE 19—		PARTICULARS	P.R.	DEBIT	CREDIT

 Name________________________ Date________________

ANSWERS TO SECTION 9.3 EXERCISES (cont.)

Ex. 3 (cont.)

Account	Debit	Credit
Bank	1 057.60	
Accounts Rec'l	9357.00	
Supplies	3 746.00	
Ppd. Insurance	3 750.00	
Tapes and Records	8 747.00	
Sound Equipment	18 800.26	
Truck	9 065.00	
Accounts Payable		2 016.50
Bank Loan		5 000.00
R. Koehler, Capital		57 773.77
R. Koehler, Drawings	10 000.00	
Revenue Admissions		41 375.00
Revenue Concessions		15 960.00
Advertising Exp.	2 740.00	
Bank Charges Exp.	742.00	
Concession Cost Exp.	15 376.10	
Light and Heat Exp.	3 431.01	
Misc. Exp.	547.30	
Musicians' Fees Exp.	4 316.00	
Rent Exp.	12 000.00	
Wages Exp.	18 450.00	
Supplies Expense		
Insurance Exp.		
Tapes, Records Exp.		
Income Summary		

 Name______________________ Date________________

ANSWERS TO SECTION 9.3 EXERCISES (cont.)

Ex. 3 (cont.)

			DR.	CR.

Exercise 4, p. 289

1. Journalizing and posting the adjusting and closing entries is a routine task that can be done by any knowledgeable accounting clerk. ☐

2. All of the data required to journalize the adjusting and closing entries can be found on the work sheet. ☐

3. It can be assumed that all adjustments have been thought of once the work sheet is completed. ☐

4. The adjusting entries must be journalized and posted to bring the ledger into agreement with the figures on the financial statements. ☐

5. An explanation is needed for each individual adjusting entry being journalized. ☐

 Name________________ Date____________

ANSWERS TO SECTION 9.3 EXERCISES (cont.)

Ex. 4 (cont.)

6. The adjusting and closing entries in the journal are dated as of the end of the fiscal period. ☐
7. The closing entries can only be processed using the four-step method. ☐
8. The figures for the first closing entry (as described in the textbook) are taken from the Income Statement section, Debit column of the work sheet. ☐
9. Since revenue accounts have debit balances, credit entries are needed to close them out. ☐
10. The second closing entry (as described in the textbook) transfers the balances in the expense accounts to the Income Summary account. ☐
11. When the adjusting entries and the first two closing entries are journalized and posted, all of the accounts in the equity section of the ledger except three will have nil balances. ☐
12. A loss has been suffered if the Income Summary account has a credit balance before it is closed out. ☐
13. The first two entries in the Income Summary account are the same as the subtotals of the Income Statement section of the work sheet. ☐
14. The Income Summary account is not closed out if a loss occurs. ☐
15. A work sheet is not necessary in a computerized system because the mathematical accuracy of the figures is assured. ☐

Explanations:

Chapter 9

Name________________________ Date________________

ANSWERS TO COMPUTER REVIEW 9.4 QUESTIONS (text, p. 294)

1. ______________________________

2. ______________________________

3. a. ______________________________
   b. ______________________________
   c. ______________________________

4. ______________________________

5. ______________________________

COMMUNICATE IT (text, p. 295)

____

 Name________________ Date____________

ANSWERS TO SECTION 9 EXERCISES (text, p. 296)

Ex.ercise 1, p. 296

1.

ACCOUNTS	TRIAL BALANCE		ADJUSTMENTS		INCOME STATEMENT		BALANCE SHEET	
	DR	CR	DR	CR	DR	CR	DR	CR
Bank	1 802 50							
Accounts Receivable	13 550 —							
Supplies	2 017 —							
Prepaid Insurance	2 150 —							
Equipment	7 200 —							
Automobile	18 000 —							
Accounts Payable		4 316 —						
Luciano Massaro, Capital		33 690 92						
Luciano Massaro, Drawings	11 000 —							
Revenue from Sales		47 976 —						
Automobile Expenses	1 940 20							
Bank Charges Expense	96 —							
Light and Heat Expense	2 402 —							
Miscellaneous Expense	200 22							
Rent Expense	1 000 —							
Telephone Expense	310 —							
Wages Expense	24 315 —							
	85 982 92	85 982 92						

 Name__________________ Date______________

ANSWERS TO CHAPTER 9 EXERCISES (cont.)

Ex. 1 (cont.)

2.

 Name________________ Date________________

ANSWERS TO CHAPTER 9 EXERCISES (cont.)

Ex. 1 (cont.)

2. (cont.)

ANSWERS TO CHAPTER 9 EXERCISES (cont.)

Ex. 1 (cont.)

3.

GENERAL JOURNAL

PAGE ________

DATE 19—8		PARTICULARS	P.R.	DEBIT	CREDIT

ANSWERS TO CHAPTER 9 EXERCISES (cont.)

Ex. 1 (cont.)

4.

Bank	
1 802.50	

Accounts Payable	
	4 316.00

Luciano Massaro, Capital	
	33 690.92

Accounts Receivable	
13 550.00	

Luciano Massaro, Drawings	
11 000.00	

Supplies	
2 017.00	

Revenue from Sales	
	47 976.00

Prepaid Insurance	
2 150.00	

Automobile Expenses	
1 940.20	

Equipment	
7 200.00	

Bank Charges Expense	
96.00	

Automobile	
18 000.00	

Light and Heat Expense	
2 402.00	

Miscellaneous Expense	
200.22	

ANSWERS TO CHAPTER 9 EXERCISES (cont.)

Ex. 1 (cont.)

4. (cont.)

Rent Expense	
1 000.00	

Telephone Expense	
310.00	

Wages Expense	
24 315.00	

Supplies Expense	

5. ____

Insurance Expense	

Income Summary	

Name____________________ Date________________

ANSWERS TO SECTION 9 EXERCISES (cont.)

COMPREHENSIVE EXERCISE

Exercise 2, p. 296

1.

ACCOUNTS	TRIAL BALANCE DR	TRIAL BALANCE CR	ADJUSTMENTS DR	ADJUSTMENTS CR	INCOME STATEMENT DR	INCOME STATEMENT CR	BALANCE SHEET DR	BALANCE SHEET CR
Bank	2 750 —							
Accounts Receivable	15 317 20							
Supplies and Materials	23 795 16							
Prepaid Insurance	4 200 —							
Land	75 000 —							
Buildings	105 000 —							
Equipment	95 700 —							
Automotive Equipment	75 325 —							
Accounts Payable		9 216 42						
Bank Loan		100 000 —						
Mortgage Payable 10%		110 000 —						
R. Lucht, Capital		122 638 91						
R. Lucht, Drawings	50 000 —							
Revenue — Advertising		218 946 —						
Revenue — Circulation		91 315 —						
Bank Interest & Charges	12 150 —							
Bldg. Maintenance Exp.	3 220 —							

ANSWERS TO SECTION 9 EXERCISES (cont.)

Ex. 2 (cont.)

1. (cont.)

Account	Debit	Credit
Car Expenses	4,960.50	
Light and Heat Expense	11,350.—	
Miscellaneous Expense	5,940.13	
Mortgage Interest Expense	5,500.—	
Postage Expense	1,240.—	
Office Salaries Expense	34,319.15	
Sales Promotion Expense	2,750.—	
Truck Expense	26,334.19	
Telephone Expense	2,946.—	
Wages Expense	94,319.—	
	652,116.33	652,116.33

 Name________________ Date____________

ANSWERS TO CHAPTER 9 EXERCISES (cont.)

Ex. 2 (cont.)

2.

 Name ____________ Date ____________

ANSWERS TO CHAPTER 9 EXERCISES (cont.)

Ex. 2 (cont.)

2. (cont.)

ANSWERS TO CHAPTER 9 EXERCISES (cont.)

Ex. 2 (cont.)

3.

ANSWERS TO CHAPTER 9 EXERCISES (cont.)

Ex. 2 (cont.)

4. **GENERAL LEDGER FOR OAKVILLE JOURNAL**

Account	Debit	Credit
Bank	2 750.00	
Accounts Rec'l	15 317.20	
Supplies and Materials	23 795.16	
Prepaid Insurance	4 200.00	
Land	75 000.00	
Buildings	105 000.00	
Equipment	95 700.00	
Automotive Equipment	75 325.00	
Accounts Payable		9 216.42
Bank Loan		100 000.00
Mortgage Payable		110 000.00
R. Lucht, Capital		122 638.91
R. Lucht, Drawings	50 000.00	
Revenue – Advertising		218 946.00
Revenue – Circulation		91 315.00
Bank Interest & Chges. Expense	12 150.00	
Building Maintenance Expense	3 220.00	
Car Expenses	4 960.50	
Light and Heat Exp.	11 350.00	
Miscellaneous Exp.	5 940.13	
Mortgage Interest Exp.	5 500.00	

ANSWERS TO CHAPTER 9 EXERCISES (cont.)

Ex. 2 (cont.)

4. (cont.)

Postage Exp.
1 240.00

Office Salaries Exp.
34 319.15

Sales Promotion Exp.
2 750.00

Truck Expense
26 334.19

Telephone Expense
2 946.00

Wages Expense
94 319.00

Supplies, Mat'ls. Exp.

Insurance Expense

Income Summary

5.

 Name ______________________ Date ________________

ANSWERS TO CHAPTER 9 EXERCISES (cont.)

Exercise 3, p. 298

ACCOUNT Supplies **NO.**

DATE		PARTICULARS	P.R.	DEBIT	CREDIT	D/C	BALANCE

ACCOUNT Supplies Expense **NO.**

DATE		PARTICULARS	P.R.	DEBIT	CREDIT	D/C	BALANCE

Exercise 4, p. 298

1. ______________________________

2. ______________________________

3. ______________________________

____

4. ______________________________

5. 1) ______________________________

2) ______________________________

____

3)

____

6. ______________________________

7. ______________________________

____

ANSWERS TO CHAPTER 9 EXERCISES (cont.)

Exercise 4 (cont.)

8. 1) __________

2) __________

3) __________

Exercise 5, p. 299

1. __________

2. __________

3. __________

4. __________

5. __________

6. __________

7. __________

8. __________

Chapter 9

Name ______________________ Date ____________________

ANSWERS TO SECTION 9 EXERCISES (cont.)

USING YOUR KNOWLEDGE

Exercise 6, p. 299

ACCOUNTS	TRIAL BALANCE		ADJUSTMENTS		INCOME STATEMENT		BALANCE SHEET	
	DR	CR	DR	CR	DR	CR	DR	CR

ANSWERS TO SECTION 9 EXERCISES (cont.)

Ex. 6,(cont.)

ANSWERS TO CHAPTER 9 EXERCISES (cont.)

Exercise 7, p. 301

GENERAL JOURNAL PAGE ______

DATE 19—		PARTICULARS	P.R.	DEBIT	CREDIT

Exercise 8, p. 301

1. ______________________________

2. ______________________________

3. ______________________________

ANSWERS TO CHAPTER 9 EXERCISES (cont.)

FOR FURTHER THOUGHT

Exercise 9, p. 302

1.
2.
3.
4.
5.
6.
7.
8.
9.
10.

CASE STUDIES (text, p. 303)

Case 1 *A Mix-Up in Year-End Accounting*, p. 303

1.
2.
3.

 Name________________ Date__________

CASE STUDIES (cont.)

Case 1 (cont.)

4. ______

5. ______

6. ______

Case 2 *Once a Liability, Always a Liability?*, p. 306

1. ______

2. ______

3. ______

4. ______

Chapter 9

Name______________________ Date________________

ENTREPRENEUR Mai MacKenzie/West Vancouver Finishing School

ANSWERS TO DISCUSSION QUESTIONS (text, p. 308)

1. ____

2. ____

3. ____

4. ____

5. ____

6. ____

 Name________________________ Date__________________

Chapter 10 Subsidiary Ledger Accounting

ANSWERS TO SECTION 10.1 REVIEW QUESTIONS (text, p. 314)

Subsidiary Ledger Theory

1. ______________________________

2. ______________________________

3. ______________________________

4. ______________________________

5. ______________________________

6. ______________________________

7. ______________________________

8. ______________________________

9. ______________________________

10. ______________________________

11. ______________________________

12. ______________________________

13. ______________________________

14. ______________________________

15. ______________________________

Chapter 10

Name________________________ Date________________

ANSWERS TO SECTION 10.1 EXERCISES (text, p. 314)

Exercise 1, p. 314

1. Most office duties are handled by ______ employees under the supervision of a few ____________ employees.
2. The bookkeeping for ________ and ________ accounts is ideally suited to a division of work.
3. The accounts of customers and the accounts of creditors are taken out of the ______ and placed in separate groups.
4. These new groups of accounts are arranged ____________ .
5. The ledger of customers' accounts is known as the ______________________ .
6. The ledger of creditors' accounts is known as the ______________________ .
7. The main ledger is now called the ____________ .
8. Two accounts are opened in the general ledger to replace those that were removed. These are called ________________________ and ______________________ .
9. The balance of the Accounts Receivable account is ________ the total of all the customers' accounts in the accounts receivable ledger.
10. Each of the two new ledgers is known as a ________________ .
11. Each of the two ________ accounts in the general ledger is known as a ______________.
12. At the end of every month the subsidiary ledgers must be ________ with their respective control accounts.

ANSWERS TO SECTION 10.1 EXERCISES (cont.)

Exercise 2, p. 315

1. The value of the accounts receivable is ____________________

2. The value of the accounts payable is ____________________

3.

a.

____

____

____

ANSWERS TO SECTION 10.1 EXERCISES (cont.)

Ex. 2 (cont.)

b.

____

____

____

c.

____

____

____

 Name________________ Date________________

ANSWERS TO SECTION 10.1 EXERCISES (cont.)

Exercise 3, p. 316

1. ______

2. ______

3. ______

4. ______

5. ______

6. ______

7. ______

ANSWERS TO SECTION 10.2 REVIEW QUESTIONS (text, p. 323)

Subsidiary Ledger Systems

1. ______

2. ______

3. ______

4. ______

5. ______

6. ______

7. ______

8. ______

 Name____________________ Date________________

ANSWERS TO SECTION 10.2 REVIEW QUESTIONS (cont.)

9.

10.

11.

12.

13.

14.

ANSWERS TO SECTION 10.2 EXERCISES (text, p. 323)

Exercise 1, p. 323

1.

2.

3.

4.

5.

6.

7.

8.

9.

10.

 Name________________________ Date__________________

ANSWERS TO SECTION 10.2 EXERCISES (cont.)

Exercise 2, p. 323

 Name________________ Date__________

ANSWERS TO SECTION 10.2 EXERCISES (cont.)

Exercise 3, p. 323 (Workbook Exercise)

Complete the chart below by placing the name of the correct source document in the first column.

	IN THE SUBSIDIARY LEDGER						IN THE GENERAL LEDGER							
	SUBSIDIARY LEDGER AFFECTED		ACCOUNT INCREASED OR DECREASED		ACCOUNT DEBITED OR CREDITED		THE ACCOUNTING ENTRY WILL BE							
WHICH SOURCE DOCUMENT IS IT?							BANK		ACCOUNTS RECEIVABLE		ACCOUNTS PAYABLE		ASSET OR EXPENSE	REVENUE (SALES)
	ACCS RECL	ACCS PAYL	IN-CREASE	DE-CREASE	DEBIT	CREDIT	DEBIT	CREDIT	DEBIT	CREDIT	DEBIT	CREDIT	DEBIT	CREDIT
		✓	✓			✓						✓	✓	
	✓			✓		✓	✓			✓				
	✓		✓		✓				✓					✓
		✓		✓	✓			✓			✓			

 Name________________ Date____________

ANSWERS TO SECTION 10.2 EXERCISES (cont.)

Exercise 4, p. 324

1., 2.

ACCOUNT Adams Bros., 12 Mountain Avenue **NO.**

DATE 19 —		PARTICULARS	P.R.	DEBIT	CREDIT	D/C	BALANCE
June.	30	Inv. No. 480		67.20			
	30	507		94.20		DR	161.40

ACCOUNT Cozo & Son, 620 Main Street **NO.**

DATE 19 —		PARTICULARS	P.R.	DEBIT	CREDIT	D/C	BALANCE
June.	30	Inv. No. 512		75.65		DR	75.65

ACCOUNT A.G. Farmer, 120A Blackwell Ave. **NO.**

DATE 19 —		PARTICULARS	P.R.	DEBIT	CREDIT	D/C	BALANCE
June.	30	Inv. No. 514		315.62		DR	315.62

ANSWERS TO SECTION 10.2 EXERCISES (cont.)

Ex. 4 (cont.)

1., 2. (cont.)

ACCOUNT S.P. Handy Ltd., 75 Porter Ave. **NO.**

DATE 19 —		PARTICULARS	P.R.	DEBIT	CREDIT	D/C	BALANCE
June.	30	Inv. No. 484		216.25			
	30	511		200.22		DR	416.47

ACCOUNT R. Mortimer, 60 Hawley Crescent **NO.**

DATE 19 —		PARTICULARS	P.R.	DEBIT	CREDIT	D/C	BALANCE
June.	30	Inv. No. 470		516.25			
	30	496		621.90			
	30	505		608.36		DR	1746.51

ACCOUNT Renforth Sales, 192 Dale Place **NO.**

DATE 19 —		PARTICULARS	P.R.	DEBIT	CREDIT	D/C	BALANCE
June.	30	Inv. No. 510		137.62		DR	137.62

ACCOUNT Vista Limited, 2001 Central Ave. **NO.**

DATE 19 —		PARTICULARS	P.R.	DEBIT	CREDIT	D/C	BALANCE
June.	30	Inv. No. 515		50.–		DR	50.–

 Name ____________ Date ____________

ANSWERS TO SECTION 10.2 EXERCISES (cont.)

Ex. 4 (cont.)

1., 2. (cont.)

ACCOUNT *Williams Company, 417 Lake Street* NO.

DATE 19—		PARTICULARS	P.R.	DEBIT	CREDIT	D/C	BALANCE

3.

____

____

____

 Name________________ Date________________

ANSWERS TO SECTION 10.2 EXERCISES (cont.)

Exercise 5, p. 325

1., 2.

ACCOUNT Daiton Enterprises, 106 Fleet Street, Barbary **NO.**

DATE 19 —		PARTICULARS	P.R.	DEBIT	CREDIT	D/C	BALANCE
Sept.	30	Purchase Inv. No. 516			430 74	CR	430 74

ACCOUNT Gordon & Associates, 700 King Street, Oak City **NO.**

DATE 19 —		PARTICULARS	P.R.	DEBIT	CREDIT	D/C	BALANCE
Sept.	30	Purchase Inv. No. B7407			216 92	CR	216 92

ACCOUNT Henderson Associates, Box 65, Welton **NO.**

DATE 19 —		PARTICULARS	P.R.	DEBIT	CREDIT	D/C	BALANCE
Sept.	30	Purchase Inv. No. 16421			507 –		
	30	16907			615 –	CR	1 122 –

ANSWERS TO SECTION 10.2 EXERCISES (cont.)

Ex. 5 (cont.)

ACCOUNT Kohler, R.M., 141 Nixon Avenue, Barbary **NO.**

DATE 19 —		PARTICULARS	P.R.	DEBIT	CREDIT	D/C	BALANCE
Sept.	30	Purchase Inv. No. 615			104 70	CR	104 70

ACCOUNT North State Packaging, 1500 Middle Road, Lennox **NO.**

DATE 19 —		PARTICULARS	P.R.	DEBIT	CREDIT	D/C	BALANCE
Sept.	30	Purchase Inv. No. 901			74 87	CR	74 87

ACCOUNT Orenson & Company, 560 The Eastway, Dayson **NO.**

DATE 19 —		PARTICULARS	P.R.	DEBIT	CREDIT	D/C	BALANCE
Sept.	30	Purchase Inv. No. 1604			1046 26		
	30	1809			516 15	CR	1562 41

 Name_____________ Date_____________

ANSWERS TO SECTION 10.2 EXERCISES (cont.)

Ex. 5 (cont.)

ACCOUNT Riggs, J.B., 75 Baxter Road, Estwing NO.

DATE 19 —		PARTICULARS	P.R.	DEBIT	CREDIT	D/C	BALANCE
Sept.	30	Purchase Inv. No. 74621			502 –	CR	502 –

ACCOUNT Smithers, P.R., 106 Farr Street, Wibbling NO.

DATE 19 —		PARTICULARS	P.R.	DEBIT	CREDIT	D/C	BALANCE
Sept.	30	Purchase Inv. No. 74			57 05	CR	57 05

ACCOUNT Union Advertising, 7900 Primeau Avenue, Marks County NO.

DATE 19 —		PARTICULARS	P.R.	DEBIT	CREDIT	D/C	BALANCE
Sept.	30	Purchase Inv. No. 16352			436 21		
	30	17201			702 16		
	30	17306			518 90	CR	1657 27

Name ______________________ Date ______________

ANSWERS TO SECTION 10.2 EXERCISES (cont.)

Ex. 5 (cont.)

ACCOUNT *Wrouse & Reid, 14 Kay Street Saxton* NO.

DATE 19—		PARTICULARS	P.R.	DEBIT	CREDIT	D/C	BALANCE

3.

ANSWERS TO SECTION 10.2 EXERCISES (cont.)

Exercise 6, p. 327

4.

GENERAL LEDGER

Bank	
500	

Accounts Receivable	
1 700	

Supplies	
70	

Equipment	
4 000	

Automobiles	
10 000	

Bank Loan	
	1 000

Accounts Payable	
	1 450

C. Chen, Capital	
	14 550

C. Chen, Drawings	
200	

Revenue	
	12 400

Advertising Expense	
500	

General Expense	
130	

Light and Heat	
1 500	

Rent Expense	
1 800	

Wages Expense	
9 000	

ANSWERS TO SECTION 10.2 EXERCISES (cont.)

Ex. 6 (cont.)

4. (cont.)

ACCOUNTS RECEIVABLE LEDGER

Aube	
300	

Crozier	
200	

Elyk	
150	

Isola	
500	

Perrier	
300	

Tams	
250	

ACCOUNTS PAYABLE LEDGER

Ace Co.	
	225

Delta Co.	
	150

Galaxy Co.	
	75

Meteor Co.	
	300

Sun Co.	
	400

Venus Co.	
	300

 Name_______________ Date_______________

ANSWERS TO SECTION 10.2 EXERCISES (cont.)

Ex. 6 (cont.)

4. (cont.)

 Name ____________________ Date ____________________

ANSWERS TO SECTION 10.2 EXERCISES (cont.)

Ex. 6 (cont.)

4. (cont.)

GENERAL JOURNAL

PAGE ________

DATE		PARTICULARS	P.R.	DEBIT	CREDIT

ANSWERS TO SECTION 10.2 EXERCISES (cont.)

Ex. 6 (cont.)

4. (cont.)

GENERAL JOURNAL

PAGE ______

DATE		PARTICULARS	P.R.	DEBIT	CREDIT

ANSWERS TO SECTION 10.2 EXERCISES (cont.)

Ex. 6 (cont.)

4. (cont.)

 Name_______________ Date_______________

ANSWERS TO SECTION 10.2 EXERCISES (cont.)

Ex. 6 (cont.)

4. (cont.)

 Name________________________ Date____________________

ANSWERS TO SECTION 10.2 EXERCISES (cont.)

Exercise 7, p. 328 (Workbook Exercise)

The simplified general ledger and subsidiary ledgers of Carson Company are given below in T-accounts.

Required:

1. Ensure that the subsidiary ledgers are in balance with their respective control accounts to start with.
2. Perform the duties of the accounts receivable clerk. Select from the source documents shown below those that affect the accounts receivable and post them directly to the T-accounts in the subsidiary ledger.
3. Perform the duties of the accounts payable clerk. Select from the source documents shown below those that affect the accounts payable and post them directly to the T-accounts in the subsidiary ledger.
4. Perform the duties of the general ledger clerk. Work out the accounting entries for the source documents shown below, journalize them in a two-column general journal, and post to the T-accounts in the general ledger. Ignore dates, explanations, and sales tax.

Source Documents

No.	Document	Name	Amount	Explanation
1.	Sales invoice	Davis	$ 75	Sale on account
2.	Purchase invoice	Acme Co.	150	Advertising
3.	Cheque copy	Bell	40	Telephone
4.	Cash receipt	Cory	250	On account
5.	Sales invoice	Stone	125	Sale on account
6.	Purchase invoice	Mercury Co.	90	Rent
7.	Cash receipt	Norris	210	On account
8.	Sales invoice	Hall	300	Sale on account
9.	Cheque copy	Beard	200	Wages
10.	Cheque copy	Star	400	On account
11.	Purchase invoice	Star	315	Supplies
12.	Cash receipt	Davis	150	On account
13.	Cash sales slip	Morrison	175	Cash sale
14.	Cheque copy	Junot	311	On account
15.	Cheque copy	Xerox	300	On account
16.	Cheque copy	Dunn	200	Drawings

5. Balance the three ledgers.

ANSWERS TO SECTION 10.2 EXERCISES (cont.)

Ex. 7 (cont.)

1.

GENERAL LEDGER

Account	Debit	Credit
Bank	1200	
Accounts Receivable	1 450	
Supplies	90	
Automobiles	5 700	
Bank Loan		3 000
Accounts Payable		2 305
C. Dunn, Capital		1 375
C. Dunn, Drawings	4 000	
Revenue		16 900
Advertising Expense	1 500	
General Expense	1 140	
Wages Expense	8 500	

ANSWERS TO SECTION 10.2 EXERCISES (cont.)

Ex. 7 (cont.)

1. (cont.)

ACCOUNTS RECEIVABLE LEDGER

Cory	
350	

Davis	
450	

Hall	
100	

Lee	
125	

Norris	
210	

Stone	
215	

ACCOUNTS PAYABLE LEDGER

Acme Co.	
	219

Federal Co.	
	150

Junot Co.	
	311

Mercury Co.	
	325

Star Co.	
	400

Xerox Co.	
	900

 Name________________ Date____________

ANSWERS TO SECTION 10.2 EXERCISES (cont.)

Ex. 7 (cont.)

2.

3.

ANSWERS TO SECTION 10.2 EXERCISES (cont.)

Ex. 7 (cont.)

4.

GENERAL JOURNAL

PAGE ________

DATE		PARTICULARS	P.R.	DEBIT	CREDIT

 Name ______________________ Date ________________

ANSWERS TO SECTION 10.2 EXERCISES (cont.)

Ex. 7 (cont.)

GENERAL JOURNAL

PAGE ________

DATE		PARTICULARS	P.R.	DEBIT	CREDIT

ANSWERS TO SECTION 10.2 EXERCISES (cont.)

Ex. 7 (cont.)

5.

 Name________________ Date____________

ANSWERS TO SECTION 10.2 EXERCISES (cont.)

Ex. 7 (cont.)

5. (cont.)

 Name ____________ Date ____________

ANSWERS TO SECTION 10.3 REVIEW QUESTIONS (text, p. 332)

Customer's Statement of Account

1. ____________

2. ____________

3. ____________

4. ____________

5. ____________

6. ____________

7. ____________

8. ____________

 Name____________________ Date________________

ANSWERS TO SECTION 10.3 EXERCISES (text, p. 332)

Exercise 1, p. 332

BIWAY SUPPLY COMPANY

4000 HUNTERS TRAIL
PRINCE EDWARD, ALBERTA

Phone
123- 4567

In Account With

DATE		REFERENCE	CHARGES		CREDITS		BALANCE	

2% Interest Charged on Overdue Accounts

Exercise 2, p. 332

1. ______________________________

2. ______________________________

 Name________________________ Date__________________

ANSWERS TO SECTION 10.3 EXERCISES (cont.)

Ex. 2 (cont.)

3. ____

____

____

Exercise 3, p. 333

____

____

____

____

____

ANSWERS TO CHAPTER 10 EXERCISES (text, p. 334)

USING YOUR KNOWLEDGE

Exercise 1, p. 334

For each statement below place a "T" (for true) or an "F" (for false) in the spaces provided. For each problem, one, two, three, or four of the parts may be correct. Assume that the system described in the chapter is used.

1. An entire journal entry, for a $500 purchase invoice for supplies, is not recorded. As a result,

   a. The general ledger still balances. ☐

   b. Two accounts in the general ledger have incorrect balances. ☐

   c. The accounts payable ledger does not agree with its control account. ☐

   d. The total in the accounts payable ledger is $500 more than the balance in the control account. ☐

2. A cheque for $400 received from a customer is posted to the customer's account as a credit of $40. As a result,

   a. The general ledger does not balance. ☐

   b. The accounts receivable ledger does not agree with its control account. ☐

   c. The total of the accounts receivable ledger is greater than the balance in the control account. ☐

   d. The accounts receivable ledger equals the control account but contains one or more errors. ☐

ANSWERS TO CHAPTER 10 EXERCISES (cont.)

Ex. 1 (cont.)

3. $208 cash received from a customer is recorded correctly in the journal and ledger but is credited to the customer's account as $280. To correct this error the accountant should:

a. Credit the customer's account $72. ☐

b. Debit the customer's account $72. ☐

c. Debit the control account $72. ☐

d. Credit the control account $72. ☐

4. A sales transaction for $800 is entered in the general journal as follows:

Revenue	$800	
Accounts Receivable		$800

As a result of this entry:

a. The general ledger trial balance does not balance. ☐

b. The accounts receivable ledger disagrees with the control account by $800. ☐

c. The balance in the revenue account is incorrect by $800. ☐

d. The balance in the revenue account is incorrect by $1 600. ☐

5. A purchase invoice for $250 is posted in the accounts payable ledger as a debit. As a result,

a. The accounts payable ledger does not equal the control account. ☐

b. The difference between the accounts payable ledger and the control account is $250. ☐

c. The difference between the accounts payable ledger and the control account is $500. ☐

d. The general ledger balances. ☐

6. A debit of $1 200 is not posted to a customer's account in the accounts receivable ledger. As a result,

a. The Revenue account and the Accounts Receivable account are both incorrect. ☐

b. The general ledger remains in balance. ☐

c. The balance of the control account is greater than the total of the accounts receivable ledger by $1 200. ☐

d. The balance of the control account is smaller than the total of the accounts receivable ledger by $1 200. ☐

 Name____________________ Date_______________

ANSWERS TO CHAPTER 10 EXERCISES (cont.)

Exercise 2, p. 335

Error No.	Control Account Balance **$13 500**	Accounts Receivable Subsidiary Ledger Balance **$13 125**
1.		
2.		
3.		
4.		
5.		
True Balance		

Exercise 3, p. 336

Analysis of errors:

	Changes to Control Account Figure	Changes to Subsidiary Ledger Figure
1.		
2.		
3.		
4.		
5.		
6.		
7.		
Total Net Corrections		

ANSWERS TO CHAPTER 10 EXERCISES (cont.)

Exercise 4, p. 336

SOURCE DOCUMENT	IN THE SUBSIDIARY LEDGER						IN THE GENERAL LEDGER									
	Which subsidiary ledger is affected?		Will the account be increased or decreased?		Will the account be debited or credited?		The accounting entry will be									
							Bank		Accounts Receivable		Accounts Payable		Asset or Expense		Revenue	
	A/R	A/P	In-crease	De-crease	Dr	Cr	Dr	Cr	Dr	Cr	Dr	Cr	Dr	Cr	Dr	Cr
PURCHASE INVOICE																
CASH RECEIPT ON ACCOUNT																
SALES INVOICE																
CHEQUE COPY ON ACCOUNT																

 Name______________________ Date______________

ANSWERS TO CHAPTER 10 EXERCISES (cont.)

Exercise 5, p. 337

Analyzing the Effect of Errors

Five error situations and a response chart are given below. You are to analyze the error situations and complete the chart. In performing your analysis, keep the following in mind:

- subsidiary ledgers are posted directly from copies of source documents;
- the general ledger is posted from journal entries in the general journal;
- unless you are informed otherwise, all accounting steps are deemed to have been done correctly.

Error Situations

1.	An entire general journal entry with respect to a $200 sales invoice is not recorded.
2.	A cheque for $100 received from a customer is credited to the wrong account in the accounts receivable ledger.
3.	A cheque for $500 issued to a creditor is posted to the creditor's account as a $50 debit.
4.	An invoice for $125 is entered in the general journal as follows: Dr Accounts Receivable $135 Cr Sales $135
5.	A purchase invoice in the amount of $75 is posted in the subsidiary ledger as a debit.

Response Chart

		Situation 1.	*Situation* 2.	*Situation* 3.	*Situation* 4.	*Situation* 5.
a.	If the general ledger will be in balance and contain no errors, enter a checkmark.					
b.	If the general ledger will be in balance but will contain one or more errors, enter a checkmark.					
c.	If the general ledger will not be in balance, enter a checkmark.					
d.	If you placed a checkmark in c. above, show the amount by which it will be out of balance.					
e.	If the subsidiary ledger will be in agreement with the control account and contain no errors, enter a checkmark.					
f.	If the subsidiary ledger will be in agreement with the control account but will contain one or more errors, enter a checkmark.					
g.	If the subsidiary ledger will not be in agreement with the control account, enter a checkmark.					
h.	If you placed a checkmark in g. above, show the amount of the difference between the control account and the subsidiary ledger.					
i.	If you checked g. above, show which has the larger total, the control account or the subsidiary ledger, by entering a C or an S respectively.					

 Name__________ Date__________

ANSWERS TO CHAPTER 10 EXERCISES (cont.)

COMPREHENSIVE EXERCISE

Exercise 6, p. 337

GENERAL JOURNAL **PAGE** 76

DATE 19—		PARTICULARS	P.R.	DEBIT	CREDIT

 Name ______________ Date ______________

ANSWERS TO CHAPTER 10 EXERCISES (cont.)

Ex. 6 (cont.)

GENERAL JOURNAL

PAGE ________

DATE 19—		PARTICULARS	P.R.	DEBIT	CREDIT

 Name________________ Date________________

ANSWERS TO CHAPTER 10 EXERCISES (cont.)

Ex. 6 (cont.)

1.

GENERAL LEDGER

ACCOUNT Bank **NO.** 101

DATE 19 —		PARTICULARS	P.R.	DEBIT	CREDIT	D/C	BALANCE
Mar.	31	Forwarded				DR	1850 –

ACCOUNT Bank **NO.** 101

DATE 19 —		PARTICULARS	P.R.	DEBIT	CREDIT	D/C	BALANCE

ACCOUNT Accounts Receivable **NO.** 105

DATE 19 —		PARTICULARS	P.R.	DEBIT	CREDIT	D/C	BALANCE
Mar.	31	Forwarded				DR	7220 –

ANSWERS TO CHAPTER 10 EXERCISES (cont.)

Ex. 6 (cont.)

1. (cont.)

ACCOUNT Supplies **NO.** 110

DATE 19 —		PARTICULARS	P.R.	DEBIT	CREDIT	D/C	BALANCE
Mar.	31	Forwarded				DR	2750 –

ACCOUNT Office Equipment **NO.** 115

DATE 19 —		PARTICULARS	P.R.	DEBIT	CREDIT	D/C	BALANCE
Mar.	31	Forwarded				DR	18400 –

ACCOUNT Automobile **NO.** 120

DATE 19 —		PARTICULARS	P.R.	DEBIT	CREDIT	D/C	BALANCE
Mar.	31	Forwarded				DR	24700 –

ANSWERS TO CHAPTER 10 EXERCISES (cont.)

Ex. 6 (cont.)

1. (cont.)

ACCOUNT Accounts Payable **NO.** 205

DATE 19 —		PARTICULARS	P.R.	DEBIT	CREDIT	D/C	BALANCE
Mar.	31	Forwarded				CR	6 449 70

ACCOUNT R. Bragg, Capital **NO.** 301

DATE 19 —		PARTICULARS	P.R.	DEBIT	CREDIT	D/C	BALANCE
Mar.	31	Forwarded				CR	47 374 15

ACCOUNT R. Bragg, Drawings **NO.** 302

DATE 19 —		PARTICULARS	P.R.	DEBIT	CREDIT	D/C	BALANCE
Mar.	31	Forwarded				DR	12 000 –

ANSWERS TO CHAPTER 10 EXERCISES (cont.)

Ex. 6 (cont.)

1. (cont.)

ACCOUNT Fees Income NO. 401

DATE 19 —		PARTICULARS	P.R.	DEBIT	CREDIT	D/C	BALANCE
Mar.	31	Forwarded				CR	31 650 –

ACCOUNT Car Expenses NO. 505

DATE 19 —		PARTICULARS	P.R.	DEBIT	CREDIT	D/C	BALANCE
Mar.	31	Forwarded				DR	3 295 60

ACCOUNT Light and Heat NO. 510

DATE 19 —		PARTICULARS	P.R.	DEBIT	CREDIT	D/C	BALANCE
Mar.	31	Forwarded				DR	950 20

ACCOUNT Miscellaneous Expense NO. 515

DATE 19 —		PARTICULARS	P.R.	DEBIT	CREDIT	D/C	BALANCE
Mar.	31	Forwarded				DR	375 40

ANSWERS TO CHAPTER 10 EXERCISES (cont.)

Ex. 6 (cont.)

1. (cont.)

ACCOUNT Rent NO. 520

DATE 19 —		PARTICULARS	P.R.	DEBIT	CREDIT	D/C	BALANCE
Mar.	31	Forwarded				DR	3 000 –

ACCOUNT Telephone NO. 525

DATE 19 —		PARTICULARS	P.R.	DEBIT	CREDIT	D/C	BALANCE
Mar.	31	Forwarded				DR	516 15

ACCOUNT Wages NO. 530

DATE 19 —		PARTICULARS	P.R.	DEBIT	CREDIT	D/C	BALANCE
Mar.	31	Forwarded				DR	10 416 50

ANSWERS TO CHAPTER 10 EXERCISES (cont.)

Ex. 6 (cont.)

2., 4. **ACCOUNTS RECEIVABLE LEDGER**

ACCOUNT Blue Cab Company 16 Fox Street NO.

DATE 19 —		PARTICULARS	P.R.	DEBIT	CREDIT	D/C	BALANCE
Mar.	31	Invoice # 74		1 9 2 0 –		DR	1 9 2 0 –

ACCOUNT Champion Store 175 Main Street NO.

DATE 19 —		PARTICULARS	P.R.	DEBIT	CREDIT	D/C	BALANCE
Mar.	31	Invoice # 75		7 5 0 –		DR	7 5 0 –

ACCOUNT Oasis Restaurant 325 Second Street NO.

DATE 19 —		PARTICULARS	P.R.	DEBIT	CREDIT	D/C	BALANCE
Mar.	31	Invoice # 76		1 5 5 0 –		DR	1 5 5 0 –

ACCOUNT Village Restaurant 400 Main Street NO.

DATE 19 —		PARTICULARS	P.R.	DEBIT	CREDIT	D/C	BALANCE
Mar.	31	Invoice # 77		3 0 0 0 –		DR	3 0 0 0 –

 Name________________ Date____________

ANSWERS TO CHAPTER 10 EXERCISES (cont.)

Ex. 6 (cont.)

3., 4

ACCOUNTS PAYABLE LEDGER

ACCOUNT M. Ball, Consultant 430 Red Road, Bigtown **NO.**

DATE 19 —		PARTICULARS	P.R.	DEBIT	CREDIT	D/C	BALANCE
Mar.	31	Forwarded				CR	1 700 –

ACCOUNT R. & R. Supply 151 King Street **NO.**

DATE 19 —		PARTICULARS	P.R.	DEBIT	CREDIT	D/C	BALANCE
Mar.	31	Forwarded				CR	2 740 –

ACCOUNT Stirling Company 46 River Road **NO.**

DATE 19 —		PARTICULARS	P.R.	DEBIT	CREDIT	D/C	BALANCE
Mar.	31	Forwarded				CR	759 50

ACCOUNT Tom's Garage 705 Victoria Street **NO.**

DATE 19 —		PARTICULARS	P.R.	DEBIT	CREDIT	D/C	BALANCE
Mar.	31	Forwarded				CR	1 250 20

ANSWERS TO CHAPTER 10 EXERCISES (cont.)

Ex. 6 (cont.)

6.

	No.											

ANSWERS TO CHAPTER 10 EXERCISES (cont.)

Ex. 6 (cont.)

7.

8.

ANSWERS TO CHAPTER 10 EXERCISES (cont.)

Exercise 7, p. 339 (Workbook Exercise)

As the accountant for Cariboo Cartage, it is your responsibility to perform the accounting functions of a small business owned by P. Sol. Cariboo Cartage offers a cartage service on a cash basis as well as to a number of regular customers on a credit basis.

The three ledgers of Cariboo Cartage are set up for you in the Workbook and are shown below.

Cariboo Cartage

General Ledger Chart of Accounts and Trial Balance

June 30, 19 –

		Debit	Credit
100	Bank	$5 580 00	
105	Accounts Receivable	6 472 65	
110	Office Supplies	1 375 00	
115	Warehouse Supplies	570 00	
120	Trucks	42 500 00	
125	Equipment	11 350 65	
200	Bank Loan		$25 000 00
205	Accounts Payable		2 255 61
210	Sales Tax Payable		550 00
215	Loan Payable		14 382 67
300	P. Sol, Capital		25 660 02
305	P. Sol, Drawings		
400	Sales		
500	Bank Charges		
505	Gas and Oil Expense		
510	Insurance Expense		
515	Light and Heat Expense		
520	Miscellaneous Expense		
525	Rent Expense		
530	Telephone Expense		
535	Truck Expense		
540	Wages Expense		
		$67 848 30	$67 848 30

ANSWERS TO CHAPTER 10 EXERCISES (cont.)

Ex. 7 (cont.)

Cariboo Cartage

Accounts Receivable Trial Balance

June 30, 19 –

Adelaide Sports	65 Brody Street	No. 204		$ 1 113 00
Best Manufacturing	1210 Van Horne Ave.	No. 209		915 60
Friday's Equipment	Century Plaza	No. 186		1 675 80
Murray's Auto Supply	100 William Street	No. 210		960 15
Ward Millwork Ltd.	565 William Street	No. 201		1 808 10
				$ 6 472 65

Cariboo Cartage

Accounts Payable Trial Balance

June 30, 19 –

Hatley Equipment	112 Rupert Street	No. 375		$ 1 908 90
Westown Garage	Century Plaza	No. 1047		346 71
				$ 2 255 61

ANSWERS TO CHAPTER 10 EXERCISES (cont.)

Ex. 7 (cont.)

1. From the following source documents:
   a. Post directly to the subsidiary ledgers from the documents where applicable. The sales tax rate is five per cent.
   b. Journalize the transactions in the general journal (starting on page 36).

SOURCE DOCUMENTS

July *1* *Sales Invoices*
No. 211, Murray's Auto Supply, $280 plus sales tax of $14, $294.
No. 212, Ward Millwork Ltd., $175 plus sales tax of $8.75, $183.75.

Purchase Invoice
Hatley Equipment, No. 392, for warehouse supplies, $220.50.

Cash Sales Slip
No. 57, $125 plus sales tax of $6.25, $131.25.

Cash Receipts Summary
Friday's Equipment, re No. 186, $1 675.80.

Cheque Copies
No. 401, P. Salas, rent for July, $1 750.
No. 402, Credit Finance Corp., monthly instalment of loan payable, $1 000.

2 *Sales Invoices*
No. 213, Best Manufacturing, $520 plus sales tax $26, $546.
No. 214, Friday's Equipment, $370 plus sales tax $18.50, $388.50.

Purchase Invoice
Westown Garage, No. 1094, for truck repairs, $294.

Cash Receipts Summary
Ward Millwork Ltd., re No. 201, $1 808.10.
Adelaide Sports, re No. 204, $1 113.

Cheque Copy
No. 403, to the accountant (you), for wages, $875.

5 *Sales Invoices*
No. 215, Adelaide Sports, $125 plus sales tax of $6.25, $131.25.
No. 216, Ward Millwork Ltd., $80 plus sales tax of $4, $84.
No. 217, Best Manufacturing, $185 plus sales tax of $9.25, $194.25.

ANSWERS TO CHAPTER 10 EXERCISES (cont.)

Ex. 7 (cont.)

Cash Receipts Summary

Murray's Auto Supply, re No. 210, $960.15.

Cheque Copy

No. 404, Civic Hydro Electric, for monthly electricity, $66.

6 *Sales Invoices*

No. 218, Friday's Equipment, $325 plus sales tax of $16.25, $341.25.
No. 219, Murray's Auto Supply, $175 plus sales tax of $8.75, $183.75.

Cash Receipts Summary

Best Manufacturing, re No. 209, $915.60.
Murray's Auto Supply, re No. 211, $294.

Cheque Copy

No. 405, Hatley Equipment, on account re No. 375, $1 000.

7 *Sales Invoice*

No. 220, Adelaide Sports, $95 plus sales tax of $4.75, $99.75.

Purchase Invoices

Mercury Sales, 19 Brent Avenue, No. 74, for office supplies, $144.38.
Westown Garage, No. 1103, for gasoline and oil, $570.80.

Cash Sales Slip

No. 58, $200 plus sales tax of $10, $210.

Cash Receipts Summary

Ward Millwork Ltd., re No. 212, $183.75.

Cheque copy

No. 406, P. Sol, personal drawings, $500.

8 *Sales Invoices*

No. 221, Best Manufacturing, $120 plus sales tax of $6, $126.
No. 222, Ward Millwork Ltd., $160 plus sales tax of $8, $168.
No. 223, Murray's Auto Supply, $60 plus sales tax of $3, $63.

9 *Sales Invoice*

No. 224, Friday's Equipment, $115 plus sales tax of $5.75, $120.75.

Cash Receipts Summary

Adelaide Sports, re No. 215, $131.25.
Friday's Equipment, re No. 214, $388.50.

Cheque Copy

No. 407, to the accountant (you), for wages, $875.

ANSWERS TO CHAPTER 10 EXERCISES (cont.)

Ex. 7 (cont.)

12 *Sales Invoices*

No. 225, Best Manufacturing, $180 plus sales tax of $9, $189.
No. 226, Adelaide Sports, $70 plus sales tax of $3.50, $73.50.

Cash Receipts Summary

Best Manufacturing, re No. 213, $546.

13 *Sales Invoices*

No. 227, Ward Millwork Ltd., $75 plus sales tax of $3.75, $78.75.
No. 228, Friday's Equipment, $310 plus sales tax of $15.50, $325.50.
No. 229, Adelaide Sports, $375 plus sales tax of $18.75, $393.75.

Cash Receipts Summary

Murray's Auto Supply, re No. 219, $183.75.

Cheque Copy

No. 408, Westown Garage, re No. 1047, $346.71.

14 *Sales Invoices*

No. 230, Murray's Auto Supply, $205 plus sales tax of $10.25, $215.25.
No. 231, Best Manufacturing, $140 plus sales tax of $7, $147.
No. 232, Ward Millwork Ltd., $25 plus sales tax of $1.25, $26.25.

Purchase Invoice

Westown Garage, No. 1127, for gasoline and oil, $375.25.

Cash Sales Slip

No. 59, $180 plus sales tax of $9, $189.

Cash Receipts Summary

Best Manufacturing, re No. 217, $194.25.
Ward Millwork Ltd., re No. 216, $84.

15 *Sales Invoice*

No. 233, Adelaide Sports, $85 plus sales tax of $4.25, $89.25.

Cash Receipts Summary

Adelaide Sports, re No. 220, $99.75.
Friday's Equipment, re No. 218, $341.25.

Cheque Copies

No. 409, Buff Insurance Agency, monthly insurance payment, $100.
No. 410, Hatley Equipment, re balance of No. 375, $908.90.
No. 411, Provincial Treasurer, re sales tax for June, $550.

Bank Debit Memorandum

Hong Kong Bank, for interest on loan and service charges, $268.50.

ANSWERS TO CHAPTER 10 EXERCISES (cont.)

Ex. 7 (cont.)

16 *Sales Invoice*

No. 234, Best Manufacturing, $230 plus sales tax of $11.50, $241.50.

Cheque Copy

No. 412, to the accountant (you), for wages, $875.

19 *Sales Invoices*

No. 235, Ward Millwork Ltd., $575 plus sales tax of $28.75, $603.75.
No. 236, Murray's Auto Supply, $1 005 plus sales tax of $50.25, $1 055.25.

Purchase Invoice

Westown Garage, No. 1174, for gasoline and oil, $375.80.

Cash Receipts Summary

Best Manufacturing, re No. 221, $126.
Murray's Auto Supply, re No. 223, $63.

20 *Sales Invoices*

No. 237, Friday's Equipment, $235 plus sales tax of $11.75, $246.75.
No. 238, Ward Millwork Ltd., $205 plus sales tax of $10.25, $215.25.

Cash Sales Slip

No. 60, $75 plus sales tax of $3.75, $78.75.

Cash Receipts Summary

Adelaide Sports, re No. 226, $73.50.

Cheque Copy

No. 413, P. Sol, personal drawings, $750.

21 *Sales Invoice*

No. 239, Adelaide Sports, $255 plus sales tax of $12.75, $267.75.

Cash Receipts Summary

Ward Millwork Ltd., re No. 222, $168.
Friday's Equipment, re No. 224, $120.75.

Cheque Copy

No. 414, Receiver General for Canada, for postage stamps, $200.

22 *Sales Invoices*

No. 240, Friday's Equipment, $90 plus sales tax of $4.50, $94.50.
No. 241, Best Manufacturing, $215 plus sales tax of $10.75, $225.75.

Cheque Copy

No. 415, Magill's Office Supplies, for the cash purchase of office supplies, $85.05.

ANSWERS TO CHAPTER 10 EXERCISES (cont.)

Ex. 7 (cont.)

23 *Sales Invoice*

No. 242, Ward Millwork Ltd., $95 plus sales tax of $4.75, $99.75.

Purchase Invoices

Westown Garage, No. 1204, for gasoline and oil, $370, and truck repairs, $609, total $979.

Hatley Equipment, No. 419, for warehouse supplies, $309.75.

Cash Sales Slip

No. 61, $205 plus sales tax of $10.25, $215.25.

Cash Receipts Summary

Best Manufacturing, re No. 225, $189.

Ward Millwork Ltd., re No. 227, $78.75.

Cheque Copies

No. 416, Mercury Sales, re No. 74, $144.38.

No. 417, to the accountant (you), for wages, $875.

No. 418, to BC Telco, cash payment of monthly phone bill, $76.25.

26 *Sales Invoices*

No. 243, Murray's Auto Supply, $125 plus sales tax of $6.25, $131.25.

No. 244, Adelaide Sports, $145 plus sales tax of $7.25, $152.25.

No. 245, Ward Millwork Ltd., $50 plus sales tax of $2.50, $52.50.

Cash Receipts Summary

Best Manufacturing, re No. 231 and No. 234, $388.50.

Ward Millwork Ltd., re No. 232, $26.25.

Cash Sales Slip

No. 62, $100 plus sales tax of $5, $105.

Cheque Copies

No. 419, Westown Garage, re No. 1094 and No. 1103, $864.80.

No. 420, Hatley Equipment, re No. 392, $220.50.

27 *Sales Invoice*

No. 246, Best Manufacturing, $265 plus sales tax of $13.25, $278.25.

Cash Receipts Summary

Ward Millwork Ltd., re No. 235 and No. 238, $819.

28 *Sales Invoices*

No. 247, Adelaide Sports, $80 plus sales tax of $4, $84.

No. 248, Friday's Equipment, $200 plus sales tax of $10, $210.

No. 249, Murray's Auto Supply, $155 plus sales tax of $7.75, $162.75.

No. 250, Ward Millwork Ltd., $105 plus sales tax of $5.25. $110.25.

ANSWERS TO CHAPTER 10 EXERCISES (cont.)

Ex. 7 (cont.)

Purchase Invoice

Mercury Sales, No. 96, for office supplies, $599.55.

Cash Receipts Summary

Adelaide Sports, re No. 229 and No. 233, $483.
Friday's Equipment, re No. 228, $325.50.
Murray's Auto Supply, re No. 230, $215.25.

29 *Sales Invoice*

No. 251, Adelaide Sports, $120 plus sales tax of $6, $126.

Purchase Invoice

Westown Garage, No. 1250, for gasoline and oil, $460.

Cash Sales Slip

No. 63, $280 plus sales tax of $14, $194.

Cash Receipts Summary

Murray's Auto Supply, re No. 236, $1 055.25.

30 *Cash Receipts Summary*

Friday's Equipment, re No. 237, $246.75.

Cheque Copy

No. 421, Westown Garage, re No. 1127, $375.25.
No. 422, to the accountant (you), for wages, $875.

Sales Invoices

No. 252, Best Manufacturing, $780 plus sales tax of $39, $819.
No. 253, Ward Millwork Ltd., $375 plus sales tax of $18.75, $393.75.

2. Post from the general journal to the general ledger.
3. Balance the general ledger.
4. Balance the subsidiary ledgers with their respective control accounts.

 Name______ Date______

ANSWERS TO CHAPTER 10 EXERCISES (cont.)

Ex. 7 (cont.)

GENERAL JOURNAL PAGE ______

DATE 19—		PARTICULARS	P.R.	DEBIT	CREDIT

ANSWERS TO CHAPTER 10 EXERCISES (cont.)

Ex. 7 (cont.)

GENERAL JOURNAL PAGE ________

DATE 19—		PARTICULARS	P.R.	DEBIT	CREDIT

 Name________________ Date________________

ANSWERS TO CHAPTER 10 EXERCISES (cont.)

Ex. 7 (cont.)

GENERAL JOURNAL PAGE ________

DATE 19—		PARTICULARS	P.R.	DEBIT	CREDIT

 Name__________________ Date______________

ANSWERS TO CHAPTER 10 EXERCISES (cont.)

Ex. 7 (cont.)

GENERAL JOURNAL PAGE ________

DATE 19—		PARTICULARS	P.R.	DEBIT	CREDIT

 Name________________ Date________________

ANSWERS TO CHAPTER 10 EXERCISES (cont.)

Ex. 7 (cont.)

GENERAL JOURNAL PAGE ______

DATE 19—		PARTICULARS	P.R.	DEBIT	CREDIT

ANSWERS TO CHAPTER 10 EXERCISES (cont.)

Ex. 7 (cont.)

GENERAL JOURNAL PAGE ______

DATE 19—		PARTICULARS	P.R.	DEBIT	CREDIT

 Name ________________ Date ________________

ANSWERS TO CHAPTER 10 EXERCISES (cont.)

Ex. 7 (cont.)

GENERAL JOURNAL PAGE ________

DATE 19—		PARTICULARS	P.R.	DEBIT	CREDIT

 Name____________________ Date____________

ANSWERS TO CHAPTER 10 EXERCISES (cont.)

Ex. 7 (cont.)

GENERAL JOURNAL PAGE ________

DATE 19—		PARTICULARS	P.R.	DEBIT	CREDIT

 Name______________ Date______________

ANSWERS TO CHAPTER 10 EXERCISES (cont.)

Ex. 7 (cont.)

GENERAL JOURNAL PAGE ______

DATE 19—		PARTICULARS	P.R.	DEBIT	CREDIT

 Name______________ Date______________

ANSWERS TO CHAPTER 10 EXERCISES (cont.)

Ex. 7 (cont.)

GENERAL JOURNAL PAGE ______

DATE 19—		PARTICULARS	P.R.	DEBIT	CREDIT

 Name________________ Date________________

ANSWERS TO CHAPTER 10 EXERCISES (cont.)

Ex. 7 (cont.)

GENERAL JOURNAL PAGE ________

DATE 19—		PARTICULARS	P.R.	DEBIT	CREDIT

 Name________________ Date________________

ANSWERS TO CHAPTER 10 EXERCISES (cont.)

Ex. 7 (cont.)

GENERAL JOURNAL PAGE ______

DATE 19—	PARTICULARS	P.R.	DEBIT	CREDIT

ANSWERS TO CHAPTER 10 EXERCISES (cont.)

Ex. 7 (cont.)

GENERAL JOURNAL PAGE ________

DATE 19—	PARTICULARS	P.R.	DEBIT	CREDIT

ANSWERS TO CHAPTER 10 EXERCISES (cont.)

Ex. 7 (cont.)

GENERAL JOURNAL PAGE ________

DATE *19—*		PARTICULARS	P.R.	DEBIT	CREDIT

ANSWERS TO CHAPTER 10 EXERCISES (cont.)

Ex. 7 (cont.)

ACCOUNT Bank **NO.** 100

DATE 19—		PARTICULARS	P.R.	DEBIT	CREDIT	D/C	BALANCE
June	30		–			D	5580 —

ANSWERS TO CHAPTER 10 EXERCISES (cont.)

Ex. 7 (cont.)

ACCOUNT Bank **NO.** 100

DATE 19—	PARTICULARS	P.R.	DEBIT	CREDIT	D/C	BALANCE

ANSWERS TO CHAPTER 10 EXERCISES (cont.)

Ex. 7 (cont.)

ACCOUNT Accounts Receivable **NO.** 105

DATE 19—		PARTICULARS	P.R.	DEBIT	CREDIT	D/C	BALANCE
June	30	Balance	–			D	6 472 65

 Name______________________ Date______________

ANSWERS TO CHAPTER 10 EXERCISES (cont.)

Ex. 7 (cont.)

ACCOUNT Accounts Receivable **NO.** 115

DATE 19—		PARTICULARS	P.R.	DEBIT	CREDIT	D/C	BALANCE

ANSWERS TO CHAPTER 10 EXERCISES (cont.)

Ex. 7 (cont.)

ACCOUNT Office Supplies **NO.** 110

DATE 19—		PARTICULARS	P.R.	DEBIT	CREDIT	D/C	BALANCE
June	30	Balance	–			D	1 375 —

ACCOUNT Warehouse Supplies **NO.** 115

DATE 19—		PARTICULARS	P.R.	DEBIT	CREDIT	D/C	BALANCE
June	30	Balance	–			D	570 —

ACCOUNT Trucks **NO.** 120

DATE 19—		PARTICULARS	P.R.	DEBIT	CREDIT	D/C	BALANCE
June	30	Balance	–			D	42 500 —

ACCOUNT Equipment **NO.** 125

DATE 19—		PARTICULARS	P.R.	DEBIT	CREDIT	D/C	BALANCE
June	30	Balance	–			D	11 350 65

ACCOUNT Bank Loan **NO.** 200

DATE 19—		PARTICULARS	P.R.	DEBIT	CREDIT	D/C	BALANCE
June	30	Balance	–			C	25 000 —

 Name______________ Date______________

ANSWERS TO CHAPTER 10 EXERCISES (cont.)

Ex. 7 (cont.)

ACCOUNT Accounts Payable **NO.** 205

DATE 19—		PARTICULARS	P.R.	DEBIT	CREDIT	D/C	BALANCE
June	30	Balance	–			C	2 2 5 5 61

ANSWERS TO CHAPTER 10 EXERCISES (cont.)

Ex. 7 (cont.)

ACCOUNT Sales Tax Payable **NO.** 210

DATE 19—		PARTICULARS	P.R.	DEBIT	CREDIT	D/C	BALANCE
June	30	Balance	–			C	550 —

ANSWERS TO CHAPTER 10 EXERCISES (cont.)

Ex. 7 (cont.)

ACCOUNTS PAYABLE LEDGER

ACCOUNT Sales Tax Payable **NO.** 210

DATE 19—		PARTICULARS	P.R.	DEBIT	CREDIT	D/C	BALANCE

ACCOUNT Loan Payable **NO.** 215

DATE 19—		PARTICULARS	P.R.	DEBIT	CREDIT	D/C	BALANCE
June	30	Balance	–			C	14 382 67

ACCOUNT P. Sol, Capital **NO.** 300

DATE 19—		PARTICULARS	P.R.	DEBIT	CREDIT	D/C	BALANCE
June	30	Balance	–			–	25 660 02

ACCOUNT P. Sol, Drawings **NO.** 305

DATE 19—		PARTICULARS	P.R.	DEBIT	CREDIT	D/C	BALANCE

 Name________________ Date________________

ANSWERS TO CHAPTER 10 EXERCISES (cont.)

Ex. 7 (cont.)

ACCOUNT Sales **NO.** 400

DATE 19—		PARTICULARS	P.R.	DEBIT	CREDIT	D/C	BALANCE

 Name________________ Date________________

ANSWERS TO CHAPTER 10 EXERCISES (cont.)

Ex. 7 (cont.)

ACCOUNT Sales **NO.** 400

DATE 19—		PARTICULARS	P.R.	DEBIT	CREDIT	D/C	BALANCE

ACCOUNT Bank Charges **NO.** 500

DATE 19—		PARTICULARS	P.R.	DEBIT	CREDIT	D/C	BALANCE

ACCOUNT Gas and Oil Expense **NO.** 505

DATE 19—		PARTICULARS	P.R.	DEBIT	CREDIT	D/C	BALANCE

ACCOUNT Insurance Expense **NO.** 510

DATE 19—		PARTICULARS	P.R.	DEBIT	CREDIT	D/C	BALANCE

 Name________________________ Date__________________

ANSWERS TO CHAPTER 10 EXERCISES (cont.)

Ex. 7 (cont.)

ACCOUNT Light and Heat Expense **NO.** 515

DATE 19—		PARTICULARS	P.R.	DEBIT	CREDIT	D/C	BALANCE

ACCOUNT Miscellaneous Expense **NO.** 520

DATE 19—		PARTICULARS	P.R.	DEBIT	CREDIT	D/C	BALANCE

ACCOUNT Rent Expense **NO.** 525

DATE 19—		PARTICULARS	P.R.	DEBIT	CREDIT	D/C	BALANCE

ACCOUNT Telephone Expense **NO.** 530

DATE 19—		PARTICULARS	P.R.	DEBIT	CREDIT	D/C	BALANCE

ANSWERS TO CHAPTER 10 EXERCISES (cont.)

Ex. 7 (cont.)

ACCOUNT Truck Expense **NO.** 535

DATE 19—		PARTICULARS	P.R.	DEBIT	CREDIT	D/C	BALANCE

ACCOUNT Wages Expense **NO.** 540

DATE 19—		PARTICULARS	P.R.	DEBIT	CREDIT	D/C	BALANCE

 Name______________ Date______________

ANSWERS TO CHAPTER 10 EXERCISES (cont.)

Ex. 7 (cont.)

ACCOUNTS RECEIVABLE LEDGER

ACCOUNT Adelaide Sports 65 Brody St. **NO.**

DATE 19—		PARTICULARS	P.R.	DEBIT	CREDIT	D/C	BALANCE
June	30	Balance 204				D	1 113 —

ACCOUNT Best Manufacturing 1210 Van Horne Ave. **NO.**

DATE 19—		PARTICULARS	P.R.	DEBIT	CREDIT	D/C	BALANCE
June	30	Balance 209				D	915 60

 Name______________ Date______________

ANSWERS TO CHAPTER 10 EXERCISES (cont.)

Ex. 7 (cont.)

ACCOUNT Friday's Equipment Century Plaza **NO.**

DATE 19—		PARTICULARS	P.R.	DEBIT	CREDIT	D/C	BALANCE
June	30	Balance 186				D	1 675 80

ACCOUNT Murray's Auto Supply 100 William Street **NO.**

DATE 19—		PARTICULARS	P.R.	DEBIT	CREDIT	D/C	BALANCE
June	30	Balance 210				D	960 15

 Name ______________ Date ______________

ANSWERS TO CHAPTER 10 EXERCISES (cont.)

Ex. 7 (cont.)

ACCOUNT Ward Millwork Ltd 565 William Street **NO.**

DATE 19—		PARTICULARS	P.R.	DEBIT	CREDIT	D/C	BALANCE
June	30	Balance 201				D	1808 10

ACCOUNT **NO.**

DATE 19—		PARTICULARS	P.R.	DEBIT	CREDIT	D/C	BALANCE

ANSWERS TO CHAPTER 10 EXERCISES (cont.)

Ex. 7 (cont.)

ACCOUNTS PAYABLE LEDGER

ACCOUNT Hatley Equipment 112 Rupert Street **NO.**

DATE 19—		PARTICULARS	P.R.	DEBIT	CREDIT	D/C	BALANCE
June	30	Balance 375				C	1 908 90

ACCOUNT Mcury Sales 19 Brent Avenue **NO.**

DATE 19—		PARTICULARS	P.R.	DEBIT	CREDIT	D/C	BALANCE

ACCOUNT Westown Garage Century Plaza **NO.**

DATE 19—		PARTICULARS	P.R.	DEBIT	CREDIT	D/C	BALANCE
June	30	Balance 1047				C	346 71

ANSWERS TO CHAPTER 10 EXERCISES (cont.)

Ex. 7 (cont.)

ANSWERS TO CHAPTER 10 EXERCISES (cont.)

Ex. 7 (cont.)

 Name________________ Date____________

ANSWERS TO CHAPTER 10 EXERCISES (cont.)

FOR FURTHER THOUGHT

Exercise 8, p. 339

1.

2.

3.

4.

5.

6.

7.

8.

9.

10.

11.

12.

13.

14.

15.

Chapter 10

Name ____________________ Date ______________

CASE STUDIES (text, p. 340)

Case 1 *Overcoming a Lack of Control over Accounts Receivable*, p. 340

1.

2.

3.

Case 2 *Is the Policy Good or Bad?*, p. 341

1.

2.

3.

Case 3 *Evaluating the Creditworthiness of Two Companies*, p. 342

1.

2.

3.

 Name________________________ Date__________________

CASE STUDIES (cont.)

4. ____
____
____
____
____

5. ____
____

ENTREPRENEUR Sylvia Kish/Sylvia Kish Wardrobes

ANSWERS TO DISCUSSION QUESTIONS (text, p. 344)

1. ____
2. ____
3. ____
4. ____
5. ____
6. ____
7. ____

 Name______________________ Date______________

Chapter 11 Accounting for a Merchandising Business

ANSWERS TO SECTION 11.1 REVIEW QUESTIONS (text, p. 350)

The Merchandising Business

1. ____
____
2. ____
3. ____
____
4. ____
____
5. ____
6. ____
7. ____
8. ____
9. ____
____
10. ____
____
11. ____
12. ____
    1) ____
    2) ____
    3) ____
    4) ____
13. ____
14. ____
____

Chapter 11

Name________________________ Date________________________

ANSWERS TO SECTION 11.1 EXERCISES (text, p. 350)

Exercise 1, p. 350 (Workbook Exercise)

For each of the following, indicate the INCORRECT statement by placing a checkmark in the appropriate box.

1. A merchandising business
   - a. is one that buys from retailers and sells to wholesalers. ☐
   - b. is one that buys from manufacturers and sells to the public. ☐
   - c. is one that buys goods for the purpose of selling them at a profit. ☐
   - d. is one that has a merchandise inventory. ☐
   - e. is one that sells goods rather than a service. ☐
2. Merchandise inventory
   - a. is stored on the shelves of a drugstore. ☐
   - b. and supplies are the same thing. ☐
   - c. is different for different businesses. ☐
   - d. represents the goods that the business deals in. ☐
   - e. is listed on the balance sheet. ☐
3. The total goods available for sale during the fiscal period is
   - a. equal to the opening inventory plus the purchases. ☐
   - b. the closing inventory plus the cost of goods sold. ☐
   - c. a current asset on the balance sheet. ☐
   - d. either on hand or not on hand at the end of the fiscal period. ☐
   - e. not shown on the balance sheet. ☐
4. Merchandise inventory
   - a. is also called stock-in-trade. ☐
   - b. consists of wood and wood products for a lumber company. ☐
   - c. is often stolen from stores. ☐
   - d. is usually a large figure on the balance sheet. ☐
   - e. is listed at selling prices in accordance with generally accepted accounting principles. ☐

ANSWERS TO SECTION 11.1 EXERCISES (cont.)

Ex. 1 (cont.)

5. Cost of goods sold

a. is usually the largest expense of a merchandising business. ☐

b. is subtracted from the sales figure to arrive at the gross profit. ☐

c. is calculated at cost prices in accordance with generally accepted accounting principles. ☐

d. is shown on the cash register tape if the business has a computerized inventory system. ☐

e. would not appear on the income statement of a service business. ☐

6. The perpetual inventory method

a. produces the quantities on hand of all of the items in stock on a daily basis. ☐

b. can only work in a business that has a computerized accounting system. ☐

c. allows a business to prepare financial statements whenever it needs to. ☐

d. is used primarily by businesses that need up-to-the-minute information regarding their inventory. ☐

e. is usually more costly than the periodic method. ☐

7. The periodic method

a. is more suitable for small businesses than the perpetual inventory method. ☐

b. makes no attempt to keep inventory data up to date. ☐

c. has been the more commonly used method over the years. ☐

d. makes it necessary to calculate the cost of goods sold by means of a formula. ☐

e. requires a business to have more stock on hand because there is no way to know the quantities on hand. ☐

8. a. The cost price of the ending inventory is listed on the balance sheet. ☐

b. The selling price of the goods available for sale is listed on the income statement. ☐

c. The selling price of the goods sold is listed on the income statement. ☐

d. The cost price of the goods sold is listed on the income statement. ☐

e. The total goods available for sale is equal to the goods sold plus the goods not sold. ☐

ANSWERS TO SECTION 11.1 EXERCISES (cont.)

Ex. 1 (cont.)

9. a. Beginning inventory + merchandise purchased = merchandise sold + ending inventory. ☐

b. Beginning inventory = ending inventory + merchandise sold – merchandise purchased. ☐

c. Beginning inventory + merchandise purchased – ending inventory = merchandise sold. ☐

d. Ending inventory = merchandise purchased – merchandise sold + beginning inventory. ☐

e. Ending inventory = beginning inventory + merchandise sold – merchandise purchased. ☐

10. a. A physical inventory is absolutely necessary when the periodic method is used. ☐

b. The physical inventory is converted into dollars and appears on the balance sheet as a current asset. ☐

c. The physical inventory figure is also the cost of goods sold figure that appears on the income statement. ☐

d. To take a physical inventory, it is often necessary to close down the store or plant for a short time. ☐

e. The periodic inventory method has been popular because it is less costly than the perpetual inventory method. ☐

Exercise 2, p. 350

Business	Inventory Items
Auto dealer	
Builder's supply dealer	
Furniture and appliance store	
Sports store	
Grocery store	
Hardware store	
Photography store	
Electronic store	
Department store	

ANSWERS TO SECTION 11.1 EXERCISES (cont.)

Exercise 3, p. 351 (Workbook Exercise)

Complete the chart by filling in the blank spaces.

	Selling price	*Cost price*	*Gross profit*	*Cost of goods sold as a % of selling price*	*Gross profit as a % of selling price*
Easy	$ 250	$	$ 100	%	%
	$	$ 85	$ 40	%	%
	$ 80	$ 56	$	%	%
	$	$ 75	$ 75	%	%
	$ 300	$ 195	$	%	%
	$ 225	$	$ 63	%	%
More difficult	$	$ 54	$	%	40 %
	$ 500	$	$	70 %	%
	$ 200	$	$	65 %	%
	$	$ 120	$	%	52 %

Exercise 4, p. 351

1.

	Year 1	*Year 2*	*Year 3*
Beginning inventory	100 units	units	units
Merchandise purchased	units	900 units	units
Goods available for sale	800 units	units	units
Merchandise sold	units	1 000 units	800 units
Ending inventory	300 units	units	50 units

2.

Cost of Goods Sold

ANSWERS TO SECTION 11.1 EXERCISES (cont.)

Exercise 5, p. 351

	Sales	Beginning Inventory	Purchases	Ending Inventory	Cost of Goods Sold	Gross Profit
1.	$125 000	$32 000	$74 250	$33 500		
2.	$750 585	$85 600	$410 360	$88 300		
3.	$288 635	$65 550	$110 357	$60 548		
4.	$174 000	$33 800	$82 640	$33 500		
5.	$255 324	$48 500	$150 650	$50 300		

Exercise 6, p. 351

2. **Cost of Goods Sold Calculation**

Exercise 7, p. 352

1.
2.
3.
4.
5.
6.
7.

 Name________________________ Date__________________

ANSWERS TO SECTION 11.2 REVIEW QUESTIONS (text, p. 355)

Accounting Procedures for a Merchandising Business

1. ______________________________

2. ______________________________

3. ______________________________

4. ______________________________

5. ______________________________

6. ______________________________

7. ______________________________

8. ______________________________

9. ______________________________

10. ______________________________

11. ______________________________

12. **a.** ______________________________

b. ______________________________

c. ______________________________

d. ______________________________

 Name______________ Date______________

ANSWERS TO SECTION 11.2 EXERCISES (text, p. 355)

Exercise 1, p. 355

GENERAL JOURNAL   PAGE ________

DATE 19—		PARTICULARS	P.R.	DEBIT	CREDIT

ANSWERS TO SECTION 11.2 EXERCISES (cont.)

Exercise 2, p. 355 (Workbook Exercise)

From the following list of transactions for Plumbing Supply House, in a two-column general journal record the transactions that affect the purchase, sale, or transportation of merchandise.

Transactions

1. *Sales Invoice*
   — No. 6024, to P. Hamblin, for sale of plumbing supplies, $572.
2. *Cheque Copy*
   — No. 174, to Jankowski Bros., $575.40 on account.
3. *Purchase Invoice*
   — From Crane Fixtures, No. 767, for sink units, $3 742.50.
4. *Cash Receipt*
   — From R. Parker, $200 on account.
5. *Cash Sales Slip*
   — No. 371, to B. Mcleod, for plumbing supplies, $74.74.
6. *Sales Invoice*
   — No. 6137, to R. Slaughter, for sale of plumbing supplies, $361.76.
7. *Cheque Copy*
   — No. 362, for wages, $1 250.
8. *Purchase Invoice*
   — From Maki Transport, No. 520, for transportation charges on incoming merchandise, $264.60.
9. *Purchase Invoice*
   — From Asco Supply, No. 802, for shower units, $2 750.
10. *Cheque Copy*
    — No. 402, to The Standard Company, for the cash purchase of plumbing supplies, $751.02.
11. *Purchase Invoice*
    — From Bass Lake Garage, No. 327, for gas and oil used in the delivery truck, $324.70.
12. *Cash Sales Slip*
    — No. 414, to W. Kell, for plumbing supplies, $125.37.
13. *Cash Receipt*
    — From J. Farino, $315.70 on account.
14. *Purchase Invoice*
    — From P. Koch, No. 614, for office supplies, $316.20.

ANSWERS TO SECTION 11.2 EXERCISES (cont.)

Ex. 2 (cont.)

GENERAL JOURNAL

DATE		PARTICULARS	P.R.	DEBIT	CREDIT

 Name ______________________ Date ______________________

ANSWERS TO SECTION 11.2 EXERCISES (cont.)

Exercise 3, p. 356

1. The final inventory figure appears on the ______________ and on the ______________.
2. Neither the ______________ nor the ______________ is known during the accounting period.
3. The cost of goods sold figure is __________ using a ________.
4. Merchandise inventory is kept in two accounts. These are: the ______________ and the ______________.
5. The ______________ normally shows the merchandise inventory figure as of the ______________.
6. At the fiscal year-end, the inventory is counted and valued at __________.
7. The Merchandise Inventory account is adjusted ______________.
8. The ______________ is the only accounting entry made to the Merchandise Inventory account.
9. Merchandise purchased during the fiscal period is debited to the ______________.
10. The "Purchases" account is a short form of ______________.
11. If merchandise is purchased on account, the account debited is __________.
12. If a tire company purchases office supplies, the account debited is __________.
13. For a merchandising business, the sales account is the __________.
14. When a business using the periodic inventory method sells goods, there is no accounting entry to record the ______________.
15. The Freight-in account is used to accumulate ______________.

Exercise 4, p. 356

Opening Inventory	Purchases	Freight-in	Closing Inventory	Cost of Goods Sold
$20 000	$40 000	$5 000	$25 000	
$29 000	$50 000	$1 000	$30 000	
$12 000		$1 000	$15 000	$50 000
	$90 000	$8 000	$39 000	$101 000
$50 000	$100 000		$60 000	$100 000
$75 000	$200 000	$5 000		$200 000

 Name____________________ Date________________

ANSWERS TO SECTION 11.3 REVIEW QUESTIONS (text, p. 362)

Work Sheet for a Merchandising Business

1.

2.

3.

4.

5.

6.

7.

8.

9.

10.

11.

12.

13.

14.

ANSWERS TO SECTION 11.3 EXERCISES (text, p. 363)

Exercise 1, p. 363

1.

Work Sheet *Bok Trading Company* *Year Ended Dec. 31, 19—*

ACCOUNTS	TRIAL BALANCE		ADJUSTMENTS		INCOME STATEMENT		BALANCE SHEET	
	DR	CR	DR	CR	DR	CR	DR	CR
Bank	500 —							
Accounts Receivable	18 300 —							
Merchandise Inventory	39 600 —							
Supplies	2 500 —			1 200 —				
Prepaid Insurance	1 800 —			1 150 —				
Equipment	27 850 —							
Accounts Payable		7 400 —		350 —				
Sales Tax Payable		7 200 —						
R. Bok, Capital		62 890 —						
R. Bok, Drawings	10 000 —							
Sales		94 310 –						
Purchases	41 500 —		300 —					
Freight-in	950 —							
Light & heat	2 750 —							
Miscellaneous Expense	350 —		50—					

ANSWERS TO SECTION 11.3 EXERCISES (cont.)

Ex. 1 (cont.)

Rent	4800—							
Telephone	1500—							
Wages	19400—							
	171800—	171800—						
Supplies Expense			1200—					
Insurance Expense			1150—					

Chapter 11

Name______________________ Date______________

ANSWERS TO SECTION 11.3 EXERCISES (cont.)

Ex. 1 (cont.)

2.

ANSWERS TO SECTION 11.3 EXERCISES (cont.)

Ex. 1 (cont.)

3.

 Name________________ Date____________

ANSWERS TO SECTION 11.3 EXERCISES (cont.)

Ex. 1 (cont.)

4. **GENERAL JOURNAL** PAGE________

DATE 19 —		PARTICULARS	P.R.	DEBIT	CREDIT

Chapter 11

Name ______________________ Date ______________

ANSWERS TO SECTION 11.3 EXERCISES (cont.)

Exercise 2, p. 364

1.

ACCOUNTS	TRIAL BALANCE		ADJUSTMENTS		INCOME STATEMENT		BALANCE SHEET	
	DR	CR	DR	CR	DR	CR	DR	CR
Bank	520 —							
Accounts Receivable	12 680 —							
Merchandise Inventory	36 050 —							
Supplies	1 975 —							
Parts and Materials	10 350 —							
Prepaid Insurance	1 150 —							
Equipment	18 600 —							
Truck	18 000 —							
Accounts Payable		5 360 —						
Bank Loan		9 500 —						
Sales Tax Payable		320 —						
H. Rohr, Capital		48 500 —						
H. Rohr, Drawings	25 000 —							
Revenue — Sales		80 362 —						
Revenue — Service		66 215 —						

CONTINUED OVERLEAF

 Name_________________________ Date____________________

ANSWERS TO SECTION 11.3 EXERCISES (cont.)

Ex. 1 (cont.)

1. (cont.)

Account		
Bank Charges	410 —	
Freight-in	862 —	
Light and Heat	2 240 —	
Miscellaneous Expense	650 —	
Purchases	52 795 —	
Rent	3 600 —	
Telephone	1 250 —	
Truck Expense	5 825 —	
Wages	18 300 —	
	210 257 —	210 257 —

 Name ______________ Date ______________

ANSWERS TO SECTION 11.3 EXERCISES (cont.)

Ex. 2 (cont.)

2. ____

____

____

Chapter 11

Name________________________ Date________________

ANSWERS TO SECTION 11.3 EXERCISES (cont.)

Ex. 2 (cont.)

3. ____

 Name ______ Date ______

ANSWERS TO SECTION 11.3 EXERCISES (cont.)

Ex. 2 (cont.)

4. **GENERAL JOURNAL** PAGE ______

DATE 19—		PARTICULARS	P.R.	DEBIT	CREDIT

 Name ______________ Date ______________

ANSWERS TO SECTION 11.3 EXERCISES (cont.)

Ex. 2 (cont.)

4. (cont.)

GENERAL JOURNAL

PAGE ______

DATE 19—		PARTICULARS	P.R.	DEBIT	CREDIT

ANSWERS TO SECTION 11.3 EXERCISES (cont.)

Ex. 2 (cont.)

5. **GENERAL LEDGER FOR SMALL ENGINE SALES AND SERVICE**

Account	Debit	Credit
Bank	520.00	
Accounts Receivable	12 680.00	
Merchandise Inventory	36 050.00	
Supplies	1 975.00	
Parts and Materials	10 350.00	
Prepaid Insurance	1 150.00	
Equipment	18 600.00	
Truck	18 000.00	
Accounts Payable		5 360.00
Bank Loan		9 500.00
Sales Tax Payable		320.00
H. Rohr, Capital		48 500.00
H. Rohr, Drawings	25 000.00	
Revenue – Sales		80 362.00
Revenue – Service		66 215.00
Bank Charges	410.00	
Freight-in	862.00	
Light and Heat	2 240.00	
Miscellaneous Exp.	650.00	
Purchases	52 795.00	
Rent	3 600.00	
Telephone	1 250.00	
Truck Expense	5 825.00	
Wages	18 300.00	
Supplies Used		
Parts, Materials Used		
Insurance Expense		
Income Summary		

 Name____________________ Date______________

ANSWERS TO SECTION 11.3 EXERCISES (cont.)

Ex. 2 (cont.)

6. ____

Chapter 11

Name____________________ Date________________

ANSWERS TO SECTION 11.3 EXERCISES (cont.)

Exercise 3, p. 365

1. GENERAL JOURNAL PAGE ________

DATE *19—*		PARTICULARS	P.R.	DEBIT	CREDIT

ANSWERS TO SECTION 11.3 EXERCISES (cont.)

Ex. 3 (cont.)

2. **GENERAL LEDGER FOR BARBINI STONE PRODUCTS**

Account	Debit	Credit
Bank	3 250.00	
Accounts Receivable	34 650.10	
Merchandise Inventory	43 700.00	
Supplies	3 400.50	
Prepaid Insurance	2 090.00	
Land	35 000.00	
Building	95 000.00	
Equipment	53 400.00	
Trucks	76 000.00	
Accounts Payable		42 375.40
Sales Tax Payable		1 354.80
T. Barbini, Capital		266 079.05
T. Barbini, Drawings	36 000.00	
Sales		232 250.00
Advertising	2 570.00	
Freight-in	3 705.00	
Light and Heat	12 316.00	
Miscellaneous Expense	1750.00	
Purchases	80 702.50	
Telephone	1 250.00	
Wages	57 275.15	
Supplies Expense		
Insurance Expense		
Income Summary		

ANSWERS TO SECTION 11.3 EXERCISES (cont.)

Ex. 3 (cont.)

3.

 Name ______________________ Date ________________

ANSWERS TO SECTION 11.4 REVIEW QUESTIONS (text, p. 373)

Merchandise Returns and Allowances

1. ______________________________

2. ______________________________

3. ______________________________

4. ______________________________

5. ______________________________

6. ______________________________

7. ______________________________
   1) ______________________________
   2) ______________________________
   3) ______________________________

8. ______________________________

9. ______________________________

10. ______________________________

11. ______________________________

12. ______________________________

13. ______________________________

 Name______________________ Date________________

ANSWERS TO SECTION 11.4 REVIEW QUESTIONS (cont.)

14. ____

15. ____

ANSWERS TO SECTION 11.4 EXERCISES (text, p. 373)

Exercise 1, p. 373

1. ____
2. ____
3. ____
4. ____
5. ____
6. ____
7. ____

Exercise 2, p. 375

ANSWERS TO SECTION 11.4 EXERCISES (cont.)

Exercise 3, p. 375 (Workbook Exercise)

Examine the two source documents below and answer the questions that follow:

Document A

WOODS WHOLESALE

NEWCASTLE, NEW BRUNSWICK

SOLD TO: Hanover Hardware
400 Hanover Street
Newcastle, N.B.
E2V 1H4

INVOICE NUMBER 365
DATE July 9, 19--
TERMS Net 30 days

Quantity	Description	Unit Price	Amount
4	3" Belt Sander	*$210.00*	*$840.00*
6	3/8 Reversible Drill	*180.00*	*1080.00*
			$1920.00

Document B

WOODS WHOLESALE

NEWCASTLE, NEW BRUNSWICK

SOLD TO: Hanover Hardware
400 Hanover Street
Newcastle, N.B.
E2V 1H4

INVOICE NUMBER 402
DATE July 17, 19--
TERMS Net 30 days

CREDIT

Quantity	Description	Unit Price	Amount
2	3" Belt Sander (returned defective)	*$210.00*	*$420.00*

Chapter 11

Name______________________ Date______________

ANSWERS TO SECTION 11.4 EXERCISES (cont.)

Ex. 3 (cont.)

1. Using returns and allowances accounts, journalize the accounting entries for both source documents as if you were the accountant for Woods Wholesale.

2. Using returns and allowances accounts, journalize the accounting entries for both source documents as if you were the accountant for Hanover Hardware.

 Name________________ Date________________

ANSWERS TO SECTION 11.4 EXERCISES (cont.)

Exercise 4, p. 375

1. ________________

2. ________________

3. ________________

4. ________________

5. ________________

6. ________________

7. ________________

ANSWERS TO SECTION 11.4 EXERCISES (cont.)

Exercise 5, p. 376

 Name______________________ Date________________

ANSWERS TO SECTION 11.5 REVIEW QUESTIONS (text, p. 379)
Perpetual Inventory

1. ____
____
2. ____
3. ____
4. ____
5. ____
6. ____
____
7. ____
____
____
____
____
8. ____
____
____
9. ____
10. ____
____
11. ____
12. ____
13. ____

ANSWERS TO SECTION 11.5 EXERCISES (text, p. 380)

Exercise 1, p. 380

1. Competition forces department stores to use the perpetual inventory system. ☐
2. The periodic inventory system produces information not possible with the perpetual inventory system. ☐
3. The copies of receiving reports are the source documents for data entry to increase the perpetual inventory. ☐
4. Deductions from the perpetual inventory are made only through the cash register in a computerized perpetual inventory system. ☐
5. In a computerized inventory system each inventory item is given a special code number. ☐

 Name________________ Date____________

ANSWERS TO SECTION 11.5 EXERCISES (cont.)

Ex. 1 (cont.)

6. There is no reason to take a physical inventory in a computerized perpetual inventory system. ☐

7. Any differences between the book figures and the manual count figures in a perpetual inventory system require a correction to the book figures. ☐

8. Given the unique code for an item, the computer can give back any information about the item that is stored in its memory. ☐

9. In a computer-produced inventory system, goods are ordered when the quantity on hand becomes less than the maximum required. ☐

10. A computerized inventory system provides management with immediate feedback, making it unnecessary to solve problems. ☐

Explanations

____

____

____

____

____

____

____

____

____

____

Exercise 2, p. 380

1. __________ forces department stores to use the perpetual inventory system.

2. The __________ inventory system produces information not possible with the ________ inventory system.

3. Additions to inventory are usually made from copies of __________ .

4. Deductions from inventory are usually made from copies of __________ or through ________ __________ in a modern store.

5. In a computerized inventory system each inventory item is given a __________ .

6. Even in a computerized inventory system a ______of stock is necessary.

7. Any differences between the _____ figure and the actual figure require an __________ to the book figure.

ANSWERS TO SECTION 11.5 EXERCISES (cont.)

Ex. 2 (cont.)

8. Given the unique code for an item, the computer can give back any information about the item that is ______ in its _______ .

9. A computer-produced inventory status report makes it possible to compare the inventory on hand with suggested _________ and _________ quantities.

10. A computerized inventory system provides management with _________ feedback which it can use to _____ problems.

Exercise 3, p. 381

1.

INVENTORY CONTROL CARD

STOCK NO. 730-0320

DESCRIPTION SCHAEFER CHEEK BLOCK — MAXIMUM 30

LOCATION: ROW 16 — BIN 3 — MINIMUM 10

DATE	REFERENCE	UNIT COST	RECEIVED	SHIPPED	BALANCE
Feb. 20	Forward	15.50			28
26	SO 904			5	23

INVENTORY CONTROL CARD

STOCK NO. 713-3011

DESCRIPTION BARTON CAM CLEAT — MAXIMUM 50

LOCATION: ROW 20 — BIN 14 — MINIMUM 20

DATE	REFERENCE	UNIT COST	RECEIVED	SHIPPED	BALANCE
Feb. 24	Forward	9.20			37
28	SO 910			10	27

ANSWERS TO SECTION 11.5 EXERCISES (cont.)

Ex. 3 (cont.)

2. ____________________

Exercise 4, p. 382

1.

THE WALTON COMPANY
INCOME STATEMENT
YEARS ENDED DECEMBER 31, 19–8 AND 19–9

	19–8	19–9
Sales	$100 000	$120 000
Cost of Goods Sold		
Opening Inventory	$ 20 000	$ 25 000
Purchases	$	$
Goods Available for Sale	$	$ 63 000
Less Closing Inventory	25 000	
Cost of Goods Sold	$	$
Gross Income	$ 65 000	$
Expenses	$	$ 37 000
Net Income	$ 33 000	$ 42 000

2. a. ____________________
b. ____________________

3. ____________________

ANSWERS TO SECTION 11.5 EXERCISES (cont.)

Exercise 5, p. 383

Shown below are some of the accounts (in T-account form) from the ledger of Beaver Trading Company. Beaver Trading Company has a computer accounting system and is able to keep its inventory and cost of goods accounts up to the minute. There is no account for Purchases. Assume that the bank account has a balance of $40 000.

Bank	
40 000	

Sales	

Merchandise Inventory	
50 000	

Cost of Goods Sold	

Record the journal entries for the following transactions directly into the ledger accounts. Ignore freight-in and sales tax.

Transactions

1. Purchased merchandise for cash at a cost of $10 000.
2. Sold goods for cash. The goods, recorded in the inventory at $6 000, are sold for $11 000. (There are two aspects of this transaction to record.)
3. Sold goods for cash. The goods, recorded in the inventory at $9 000, are sold for $15 000. (There are two aspects of this transaction to record.)
4. Purchased merchandise for cash at a cost of $3 000.

 Name ____________ Date ____________

ANSWERS TO CHAPTER 11 EXERCISES (text, p. 385)

USING YOUR KNOWLEDGE

Exercise 1, p. 385

GENERAL JOURNAL

PAGE ______

DATE 19—		PARTICULARS	P.R.	DEBIT	CREDIT

ANSWERS TO CHAPTER 11 EXERCISES (cont.)

Ex. 1 (cont.)

GENERAL JOURNAL

PAGE ______

DATE 19—		PARTICULARS	P.R.	DEBIT	CREDIT

 Name__________ Date__________

ANSWERS TO CHAPTER 11 EXERCISES (cont.)

Ex. 1 (cont.)

GENERAL JOURNAL

PAGE ________

DATE 19—		PARTICULARS	P.R.	DEBIT	CREDIT

 Name________________ Date________________

ANSWERS TO CHAPTER 11 EXERCISES (cont.)

Ex. 1 (cont.)

GENERAL JOURNAL

PAGE ________

DATE 19__		PARTICULARS	P.R.	DEBIT	CREDIT

ANSWERS TO CHAPTER 11 EXERCISES (cont.)

Exercise 2, p. 386 (Workbook Exercise)

Inter-City Electronics is a business in Fredericton, N.B., owned by J. Greer. The chart of accounts for Inter-City Electronics is given below:

Inter-City Electronics
Chart of Accounts

Bank	Sales
Accounts Receivable	Advertising
Supplies	Bank Charges
Prepaid Insurance	Freight-in
Land	Gas and Oil Expense
Building	Insurance Expense
Equipment	Light and Heat
Automotive Equipment	Miscellaneous Expense
Accounts Payable	Mortgage Interest
Sales Tax Payable	Purchases
Bank Loan	Purchases Returns and Allowances
Mortgage Payable	Repairs and Maintenance
J. Greer — Capital	Salaries
J. Greer — Drawings	Supplies Expense
Sales	Telephone
	Wages

In a two-column general journal starting on p. 97 record the accounting entries for the transactions below.

Transactions

June 2 *Cheque Copy No. 852*
— Issued to the owner for personal use; $700.

3 *Cash Receipt*
— Received from P. Lewicki in payment of his account balance; $352.25.

4 *Sales Invoice 14522*
— Issued to KBM Television for sale of merchandise on account; $353.00 with no sales tax.

5 *Sales Invoice No. 14523*
— Issued to R. Willis for sale of merchandise on account; $500 plus 7% sales tax, total $535.

6 *Purchase Invoice*
— Received from Marconi Company for merchandise for resale; $1 525.

9 *Credit Invoice No. 14524*
— Issued to Court Street Medical Clinic for return of defective goods; $450 plus 7% sales tax, total $481.50.

10 *Cheque Copy No. 853*
— Issued to Central Mortgage for the monthly mortgage payment, $389.86 principal reduction, $302.15 interest, total $692.01.

11 *Cash Sales Slip No. 5602*
— Issued to W. Yoller for the cash sale of merchandise; $425 plus 7% sales tax, total $454.75.

ANSWERS TO CHAPTER 11 EXERCISES (cont.)

Ex. 2 (cont.)

12 *Credit Invoice Received*
— Received from Toshiba Corporation for merchandise returned; $2 478.00.

13 *Memorandum*
— From the owner to the effect that he collected $500 on account from P. Slaught, a customer, and kept the money for his own personal use.

16 *Purchase Invoice*
— Received from Stark Insurance Brokers for insurance on the building for three years; $478.

17 *Purchase Invoice*
— Received from Harry's Trucking for transportation charges on incoming merchandise; $256.

18 *Cash Receipt*
— Received from KBM Television in payment of the sale made to them on June 4 above.

19 *Cheque Copy No. 854*
— Issued to Marconi Company in payment of the bill received on June 6 above.

20 *Cheque Copy No. 855*
— Issued to Local Hydro for cash payment of the hydro bill for the month; $98.35.

23 *Sales Invoice No. 14525*
— Issued to Northland Maintenance for merchandise sold on account: $575 plus 7% sales tax, total $615.25.

24 *Bank Advice*
— For the bank interest and charges for one month; $87.50.

25 *Memorandum*
— Received from the auditor stating that a purchase invoice previously debited to Buildings should have been charged to Repairs and Maintenance; $356.

26 *Cheque Copy No. 856*
— Issued to the Provincial Treasurer in payment of the sales tax for the previous month; $856.25 plus penalty of $25 for late remittance, total $881.25.

27 *Gasoline Credit Card Statement*
— Received from Petrocan for gasoline purchases; $426.35.

30 *Purchase Invoice*
— Received from Imperial Supply, for Merchandise for resale, $525; for supplies, $265.36; total $790.36.

 Name ______________ Date ______________

ANSWERS TO CHAPTER 11 EXERCISES (cont.)

Ex. 2 (cont.)

GENERAL JOURNAL

PAGE ________

DATE 19 —		PARTICULARS	P.R.	DEBIT	CREDIT

ANSWERS TO CHAPTER 11 EXERCISES (cont.)

Ex. 2 (cont.)

GENERAL JOURNAL

PAGE ______

DATE 19 —		PARTICULARS	P.R.	DEBIT	CREDIT

ANSWERS TO CHAPTER 11 EXERCISES (cont.)

Ex. 2 (cont.)

GENERAL JOURNAL PAGE ______

DATE 19 —		PARTICULARS	P.R.	DEBIT	CREDIT

 Name______________ Date______________

ANSWERS TO CHAPTER 11 EXERCISES (cont.)

Ex. 2 (cont.)

GENERAL JOURNAL

PAGE ________

DATE 19—		PARTICULARS	P.R.	DEBIT	CREDIT

 Name________________ Date______________

ANSWERS TO CHAPTER 11 EXERCISES (cont.)

Ex. 2 (cont.)

GENERAL JOURNAL

PAGE ________

DATE 19—		PARTICULARS	P.R.	DEBIT	CREDIT

Exercise 3, p. 386

Indicate whether each of the following statements is true or false by placing a "T" or an "F" in the space indicated. Explain the reason for each "F" response in the space provided.

1. A "wholesaler" is a "merchandiser." Therefore, a "merchandiser" is a "wholesaler." ☐
2. Some of the goods found in the inventory of a hardware store are also goods found in the inventory of a building supply store. ☐
3. Merchandise inventory is on the balance sheet under Prepaid Expenses. ☐
4. The cost of goods sold figure normally includes the cost of goods that are lost, stolen, or broken. ☐
5. The merchandise inventory of a drug store is calculated by counting all of the goods on hand and multiplying by the selling prices marked on the goods. ☐
6. An item that cost $40 and sold for $80 produced a gross profit of 50 per cent of the selling price. ☐
7. The difference between the selling price and the cost price of the goods for a fiscal period is also the net income figure before deducting any operating expenses. ☐
8. The goods not sold represent the ending inventory. ☐
9. The goods sold at selling prices represent the revenue figure. ☐
10. The perpetual inventory system has not been commonly used because of the amount of work required to keep track of the many individual items in the inventory. ☐

ANSWERS TO CHAPTER 11 EXERCISES (cont.)

Ex. 3 (cont.)

11. A used car business could easily use the perpetual inventory system because the number of items in its inventory is quite small. ☐

12. XYZ department store uses the periodic inventory method. It must take a physical inventory at least once a year. ☐

13. A perpetual inventory results in a "calculated" inventory figure. The inventory quantities shown on a perpetual inventory listing should be checked by actually inspecting the inventory from time to time. This would make clear whether or not any goods were stolen. ☐

14. If the beginning inventory was 10 000 units and the ending inventory was 12 000 units, the business sold more units than it purchased. ☐

15. The merchandise inventory figure can be found during the fiscal period from the Merchandise Inventory Account. ☐

16. The Purchases account is used to accumulate all purchases during the period. ☐

17. When a business that uses the periodic method sells goods, no accounting entry is made to reduce the merchandise inventory. If it were made, this entry would be debit Cost of Goods Sold and credit Merchandise Inventory. ☐

18. The Freight-in account is used to accumulate all transportation charges during the fiscal period. ☐

19. Freight-in is considered to be a cost of the goods acquired. ☐

20. On the work sheet the Purchases figure in the trial balance is extended to the Income Statement section, Debit column. ☐

21. On the work sheet the Merchandise Inventory figure in the trial balance is extended to the Balance Sheet section, Debit column. ☐

22. Both the beginning and the ending inventory figures are shown on the income statement of a merchandising company. ☐

23. The Merchandise Inventory account is automatically adjusted by the closing entries. ☐

24. A credit invoice is issued by the vendor and received by the buyer. ☐

ANSWERS TO CHAPTER 11 EXERCISES (cont.)

Ex. 3 (cont.)

25. The accounting entry for a credit note issued is either:

	DR	CR
Accounts Receivable	$$$$	
Sales		$$$$
or		
Accounts Receivable	$$$$	
Sales Returns and Allowances		$$$$

Explanations

 Name________________ Date________________

ANSWERS TO CHAPTER 11 EXERCISES (cont.)

Exercise 4, p. 387

1.

ANSWERS TO CHAPTER 11 EXERCISES (cont.)

Ex. 4 (cont.)

1. (cont.)

 Name__________ Date__________

ANSWERS TO CHAPTER 11 EXERCISES (cont.)

Ex. 4 (cont.)

2.

GENERAL JOURNAL

PAGE__________

DATE 19—		PARTICULARS	P.R.	DEBIT	CREDIT

ANSWERS TO CHAPTER 11 EXERCISES (cont.)

Exercise 5, p. 388

1.

2.

 Name________________ Date________________

ANSWERS TO CHAPTER 11 EXERCISES (cont.)

Exercise 6, p. 389

Note: The key to this exercise is that the gross profit figure is 40 per cent of the sales figure.

ANSWERS TO CHAPTER 11 EXERCISES (cont.)

Exercise 7, p. 389

Exercise 8, p. 390

1.
2.
3.
4.
5.
6.
7.

FOR FURTHER THOUGHT

Exercise 9, p. 390

1.
2.
3.
4.
5.

 Name________________ Date______________

ANSWERS TO CHAPTER 11 EXERCISES (cont.)

Ex. 9 (cont.)

6. ______________________________

7. ______________________________

8. ______________________________

9. ______________________________

10. ______________________________

11. ______________________________

12. ______________________________

13. ______________________________

14. ______________________________

15. ______________________________

17. ______________________________

18. ______________________________

19. ______________________________

20. ______________________________

Chapter 11

Name________________________ Date________________

CASE STUDIES (text, p. 391)

Case 1 *Analyzing Income Statements*, p. 391

1.

2.

3. a.

b.

Case 2 *Irregularity Disclosed by Income Statement*, p. 392

1.

2.

3.

4.

Case 3 Challenge *A Scheme To Save on Income Tax?*, p. 393

1.

2.

3.

4.

Case 4 Challenge *Understating Inventory on Tax Returns*, p. 395

Part A

1.

 Name________________ Date________________

CASE STUDIES (cont.)

Case 4 (cont.)

2. Year | 1 | 2 | 3 | 4 | 5

a. ______

b. ______

c. ______

d. ______

e. ______

f. ______

g. ______

Part B

1. ______

2. ______

3. ______

4. ______

Chapter 11

Name________________________ Date__________________

ENTREPRENEURS Gyle Graham, Guy Louis, and Su Ann Lim/ Pacific Edge Trade Group

ANSWERS TO DISCUSSION QUESTIONS (text, p. 399)

1. ____
2. ____
3. ____
4. ____
5. ____
6. ____

 Name________________________ Date________________

Chapter 12 Specialized Journals

ANSWERS TO SECTION 12.1 REVIEW QUESTIONS (text, p. 416) The Synoptic Journal

1. ______________________________

2. ______________________________

3. ______________________________

4. ______________________________
____

5. ______________________________
____

6. ______________________________

7. ______________________________
____

8. ______________________________
____

9. ______________________________
____
____

10. ______________________________
____

11. ______________________________
____

12. ______________________________
____
____

Chapter 12

Name____________________ Date________________

ANSWERS TO SECTION 12.1 EXERCISES (text, p. 416)

Exercise 1, p. 416

1. A non-routine transaction is one that is out of the ordinary. ☐
2. The synoptic journal is ideally suited to a large company. ☐
3. A synoptic journal is a multi-columnar journal. ☐
4. In the synoptic journal there would be a special column for Sales Tax Payable because it is a frequently occurring item. ☐
5. The headings in a synoptic journal are always the same as shown in the textbook. ☐
6. The main advantage of the synoptic journal is time saved in journalizing transactions. ☐
7. An advantage of the synoptic journal is that it is not necessary to balance the accounting entry for every transaction. ☐
8. The synoptic journal is balanced at the end of every month and at the end of every page. ☐
9. The accuracy of the synoptic journal is checked by cross balancing. ☐
10. The synoptic journal should be cross balanced before the final totals are inked in and the journal ruled off. ☐
11. It is customary to forward the totals from one page of the synoptic journal to the next. ☐
12. The total of the Other Accounts debit section is posted as a debit to the general ledger. ☐
13. The postings from the synoptic journal are dated the last day of the month. ☐
14. No cross-referencing is necessary when using a synoptic journal. ☐
15. A two-journal system provides a different route for non-routine transactions. ☐
16. A debit amount can be entered in a credit column if it is circled. ☐
17. Every entry in the synoptic journal takes only one line. ☐

NOTE: RECORD EXPLANATIONS ON PAGE 440.

ANSWERS TO SECTION 12.1 EXERCISES (cont.)

Exercise 2, p. 417

SYNOPTIC JOURNAL **PAGE** ______

1.

DATE	CUSTOMER/SUPPLIER	NO.	BANK		ACCOUNTS RECEIVABLE	
			DR	CR	DR	CR

WERS TO SECTION 12.1 EXERCISES (cont.)

(cont.)

MONTH OF ____________ 19 ______ PAGE ______

ACCOUNTS PAYABLE		SALES OR REVENUE	PURCHASES	SALES TAX PAYABLE	OTHER ACCOUNTS			
DR	CR	CR	DR	CR	ACCOUNT	PR	DR	CR

 Name________________ Date________________

ANSWERS TO SECTION 12.1 EXERCISES (cont.)

Ex. 1 (cont.)

Explanations

 Name________________ Date________________

ANSWERS TO SECTION 12.1 EXERCISES (cont.)

Ex. 2 (cont.)

ANSWERS TO SECTION 12.1 EXERCISES (cont.)

Exercise 3, p. 419

Shown on p. 420, in condensed form, are the synoptic journal and the T-account general ledger of Plastic Products, owned by Jean Webb.

1. Post the synoptic journal to the general ledger. Ignore dates and cross-references. Use check marks to indicate that postings are completed.
2. Take off a general ledger trial balance.

Synoptic Journal

1.

ANSWERS TO SECTION 12.1 EXERCISES (cont.)

Ex. 3 (cont.)

General Ledger

Account	Debit	Credit
Bank	70	
Accounts Receivable	350	
Merchandise Inventory	900	
Supplies	100	
Equipment	2 000	
Bank Loan		1 000
Accounts Payable		150
Sales Tax Payable		300
J. Webb Capital		3020
J. Webb Drawings	500	
Sales		4 500
Purchases	2000	
Freight-in	100	
Bank Charges	40	
Car Expenses	500	
General Expense	90	
Rent	300	
Telephone	50	
Utilities	1 220	
Wages	750	

 Name________________ Date____________

ANSWERS TO SECTION 12.1 EXERCISES (cont.)

Ex. 3 (cont.)

2.

WERS TO SECTION 12.1 EXERCISES (cont.)

cise 4, p. 420 (Workbook Exercise)

he following synoptic journal to the general ledger accounts and balance the general ledger.

SYNOPTIC JOURNAL

DATE	CUSTOMER/SUPPLIER	NO.	BANK DR	BANK CR	ACCOUNTS RECEIVABLE DR	ACCOUNTS RECEIVABLE CR	
2	Cash Sale	105	935 16				1
3	Acme Stationers						2
5	John Davidson	1295		175 –			3
6	G. Tunney	S902			337 –		4
9	Ferry Manufacturers						5
12	Jim's Gas Station						6
13	Frank Ryan	1296		500 –			7
14	Mercenary Bank		1000 –				8
18	Armstrong & Smith		372 –			372 –	9
24	Jones Supply	1297		500 –			10
25	C. Walters	1298		175 –			11
29	Gem Realty	1299		400 –			12
31	Harper Tools						13
			2307 16	1750 –	337 –	372 –	14
							15
							16

MONTH OF August 19 — PAGE 75

	ACCOUNTS PAYABLE DR	ACCOUNTS PAYABLE CR	SALES OR INCOME CR	PURCHASES DR	WAGES DR	OTHER ACCOUNTS: ACCOUNT	P.R.	DR	CR
1			935 16						
2		276 41				Supplies		276 41	
3					175 –				
4			337 –						
5		750 –		750 –					
6		62 50				Delivery Exp.		62 50	
7						F. Ryan Draw		500 –	
8						Bank Loan			1000 –
9									
10	500 –								
11					175 –				
12						Rent Exp.		400 –	
13		716 50		716 50					
14	500 –	1805 41	1272 16	1466 50	350 –			1238 91	1000 –
15									
16									

 Name______________ Date______________

ANSWERS TO SECTION 12.1 EXERCISES (cont.)

Ex. 4 (cont.)

GENERAL LEDGER

ACCOUNT Bank **NO.** 101

DATE 19—		PARTICULARS	P.R.	DEBIT	CREDIT	D/C	BALANCE
July	31	Balance	—			DR	3 000 –

ACCOUNT Accounts Receivable **NO.** 102

DATE 19—		PARTICULARS	P.R.	DEBIT	CREDIT	D/C	BALANCE
July	31	Balance				DR	500 –

ACCOUNT Merchandise Inventory **NO.** 103

DATE 19—		PARTICULARS	P.R.	DEBIT	CREDIT	D/C	BALANCE
July	31	Balance	—			DR	10 000 –

ACCOUNT Supplies **NO.** 104

DATE 19—		PARTICULARS	P.R.	DEBIT	CREDIT	D/C	BALANCE

ANSWERS TO SECTION 12.1 EXERCISES (cont.)

Ex. 4 (cont.)

ACCOUNT Bank Loan **NO.** 201

DATE 19—		PARTICULARS	P.R.	DEBIT	CREDIT	D/C	BALANCE

ACCOUNT Accounts Payable **NO.** 202

DATE 19—		PARTICULARS	P.R.	DEBIT	CREDIT	D/C	BALANCE

ACCOUNT F. Ryan, Capital **NO.** 301

DATE 19—		PARTICULARS	P.R.	DEBIT	CREDIT	D/C	BALANCE
July	31		—			CR	13 500 –

ACCOUNT F. Ryan, Drawings **NO.** 302

DATE 19—		PARTICULARS	P.R.	DEBIT	CREDIT	D/C	BALANCE

ACCOUNT Sales **NO.** 401

DATE 19—		PARTICULARS	P.R.	DEBIT	CREDIT	D/C	BALANCE

 Name________________ Date__________

ANSWERS TO SECTION 12.1 EXERCISES (cont.)

Ex. 4 (cont.)

ACCOUNT Purchases **NO.** 501

DATE 19 —	PARTICULARS	P.R.	DEBIT	CREDIT	D/C	BALANCE

ACCOUNT Delivery Expense **NO.** 502

DATE 19 —	PARTICULARS	P.R.	DEBIT	CREDIT	D/C	BALANCE

ACCOUNT Rent Expense **NO.** 503

DATE 19 —	PARTICULARS	P.R.	DEBIT	CREDIT	D/C	BALANCE

ACCOUNT Wages Expense **NO.** 504

DATE 19 —	PARTICULARS	P.R.	DEBIT	CREDIT	D/C	BALANCE

 Name________________ Date________________

ANSWERS TO SECTION 12.1 EXERCISES (cont.)

Ex. 4 (cont.)

2.

		General Ledger Trial Balance	DR.	CR.

Chapter 12

Name__________________________ Date______________

COMPREHENSIVE EXERCISE
Exercise 5, p. 421

SYNOPTIC JOURNAL

1., 2.

DATE	CUSTOMER/SUPPLIER	NO.	BANK		ACCOUNTS RECEIVABLE	
			DR	CR	DR	CR

 Name____________________ Date________________

WERS TO SECTION 12.1 EXERCISES (cont.)

(cont.) **MONTH OF**______________ **19**______ **PAGE**______

ACCOUNTS PAYABLE		SALES OR REVENUE	PURCHASES	SALES TAX PAYABLE	OTHER ACCOUNTS			
DR	CR	CR	DR	CR	ACCOUNT	P.R.	DR	CR

 Name______________________ Date______________

ANSWERS TO SECTION 12.1 EXERCISES (cont.)

Ex. 5 (cont.)

SYNOPTIC JOURNAL

DATE		CUSTOMER/SUPPLIER	NO.	BANK		ACCOUNTS RECEIVABLE		
				DR	CR	DR	CR	
								1
								2
								3
								4
								5
								6
								7
								8
								9
								10
								11
								12
								13
								14
								15
								16
								17
								18
								19
								20
								21
								22
								23
								24
								25
								26
								27
								28
								29
								30
								31
								32

WERS TO SECTION 12.1 EXERCISES (cont.)

(cont.) MONTH OF ______________ 19 ______ PAGE ______

ACCOUNTS PAYABLE		SALES OR REVENUE	PURCHASES	SALES TAX PAYABLE	OTHER ACCOUNTS			
DR	CR	CR	DR	CR	ACCOUNT			

ANSWERS TO SECTION 12.1 EXERCISES (cont.)

Ex. 5 (cont.)

ACCOUNT Bank **NO.** 101

3.

DATE 19—		PARTICULARS	P.R.	DEBIT	CREDIT	D/C	BALANCE
June	30	Forwarded	—			D	12 4 0 0

ACCOUNT Accounts Receivable **NO.** 105

DATE 19—		PARTICULARS	P.R.	DEBIT	CREDIT	D/C	BALANCE
June	30	Forwarded	—			D	13 3 6 5 2

ACCOUNT Merchandise Inventory **NO.** 110

DATE 19—		PARTICULARS	P.R.	DEBIT	CREDIT	D/C	BALANCE
June	30	Forwarded	—			D	46 0 9 0 2

ACCOUNT Supplies **NO.** 115

DATE 19—		PARTICULARS	P.R.	DEBIT	CREDIT	D/C	BALANCE
June	30	Forwarded	—			D	1 3 9 5

ACCOUNT Store Equipment **NO.** 120

DATE 19—		PARTICULARS	P.R.	DEBIT	CREDIT	D/C	BALANCE
June	30	Forwarded	—			D	20 9 0 6

 Name ____________ Date ____________

ANSWERS TO SECTION 12.1 EXERCISES (cont.)

Ex. 5 (cont.)

ACCOUNT Delivery Equipment **NO.** 130

DATE 19—		PARTICULARS	P.R.	DEBIT	CREDIT	D/C	BALANCE
June	30	Forwarded	—			D	19 500 –

ACCOUNT Accounts Payable **NO.** 201

DATE 19—		PARTICULARS	P.R.	DEBIT	CREDIT	D/C	BALANCE
June	30	Forwarded	—			C	10 265 35

ACCOUNT Sales Tax Payable **NO.** 205

DATE 19—		PARTICULARS	P.R.	DEBIT	CREDIT	D/C	BALANCE
June	30	Forwarded	—			C	2 240 –

ACCOUNT Loan Payable — Federal Finance **NO.** 210

DATE 19—		PARTICULARS	P.R.	DEBIT	CREDIT	D/C	BALANCE
June	30	Forwarded	—			C	8 550 85

ACCOUNT F. Dunn, Capital **NO.** 301

DATE 19—		PARTICULARS	P.R.	DEBIT	CREDIT	D/C	BALANCE
June	30	Forwarded	—			C	89 952 08

 Name ____________________ Date ____________________

ANSWERS TO SECTION 12.1 EXERCISES (cont.)

Ex. 5 (cont.)

ACCOUNT F. Dunn, Drawings **NO.** 302

DATE 19—		PARTICULARS	P.R.	DEBIT	CREDIT	D/C	BALANCE
June	30	Forwarded	—			D	6 000 –

ACCOUNT Sales **NO.** 401

DATE 19—		PARTICULARS	P.R.	DEBIT	CREDIT	D/C	BALANCE
June	30	Forwarded	—			C	48 585 50

ACCOUNT Delivery Expense **NO.** 505

DATE 19—		PARTICULARS	P.R.	DEBIT	CREDIT	D/C	BALANCE
June	30	Forwarded	—			D	5 258 –

ACCOUNT Freight-in **NO.** 510

DATE 19—		PARTICULARS	P.R.	DEBIT	CREDIT	D/C	BALANCE
June	30	Forwarded	—			D	956 23

ACCOUNT General Expense **NO.** 515

DATE 19—		PARTICULARS	P.R.	DEBIT	CREDIT	D/C	BALANCE
June	30	Forwarded	—			D	2 953 10

ANSWERS TO SECTION 12.1 EXERCISES (cont.)

Ex. 5 (cont.)

ACCOUNT Purchases **NO.** 520

DATE 19—		PARTICULARS	P.R.	DEBIT	CREDIT	D/C	BALANCE
June	30	Forwarded	—			D	14 120 –

ACCOUNT Rent Expense **NO.** 525

DATE 19—		PARTICULARS	P.R.	DEBIT	CREDIT	D/C	BALANCE
June	30	Forwarded	—			D	2 400 –

ACCOUNT Wages Expense **NO.** 530

DATE 19—		PARTICULARS	P.R.	DEBIT	CREDIT	D/C	BALANCE
June	30	Forwarded	—			D	14 250 –

ANSWERS TO SECTION 12.1 EXERCISES (cont.)

Ex. 5 (cont.)

ACCOUNTS RECEIVABLE LEDGER

ACCOUNT R. Lai NO.

DATE 19—		PARTICULARS	P.R.	DEBIT	CREDIT	D/C	BALANCE
June	30	Forwarded # 1407	—			D	4 072 15

ACCOUNT G. Langford NO.

DATE 19—		PARTICULARS	P.R.	DEBIT	CREDIT	D/C	BALANCE
June	30	Forwarded # 1431	—			D	6 316 20

ACCOUNT R. Potts NO. 130

DATE 19—		PARTICULARS	P.R.	DEBIT	CREDIT	D/C	BALANCE
June	30	Forwarded # 1436	—			D	2 976 90

 Name ______________________ Date ______________

ANSWERS TO SECTION 12.1 EXERCISES (cont.)

Ex. 5 (cont.)

ACCOUNTS PAYABLE LEDGER

ACCOUNT City Hardware Supply **NO.**

DATE 19 —		PARTICULARS	P.R.	DEBIT	CREDIT	D/C	BALANCE
June	30	Forwarded # 17421	—			C	6742 10

ACCOUNT Clix Oil Company **NO.**

DATE 19 —		PARTICULARS	P.R.	DEBIT	CREDIT	D/C	BALANCE

ACCOUNT Joe Jay Transport **NO.**

DATE 19 —		PARTICULARS	P.R.	DEBIT	CREDIT	D/C	BALANCE

ACCOUNT Special Steel Products **NO.**

DATE 19 —		PARTICULARS	P.R.	DEBIT	CREDIT	D/C	BALANCE
June	30	Forwarded # 147A	—			C	3523 25

Name________________________ Date________________

ANSWERS TO SECTION 12.1 EXERCISES (cont.)

Ex. 5 (cont.)

4. ____

____

____

ANSWERS TO SECTION 12.1 EXERCISES (cont.)

Ex. 5 (cont.)

5. ______________________________

Chapter 12

Name______________________ Date__________________

12.2 The Five-Journal System

ANSWERS TO SECTION 12.2 REVIEW QUESTIONS (text, p. 432) The Five-Journal System

1. ______________________________

2. ______________________________

3. ______________________________
   1) ______________________________
   2) ______________________________

4. ______________________________

5. ______________________________

6. ______________________________

7. ______________________________

8. ______________________________

9. ______________________________

10. ______________________________

11. ______________________________

12. ______________________________

Chapter 12 Name____________________ Date________________

ANSWERS TO SECTION 12.2 EXERCISES, (text, p. 432)

Exercise 1, p. 432

CASH PAYMENTS JOURNAL MONTH OF 19—

DATE	PARTICULARS	OTHER ACCOUNTS DR			WAGES DR	PURCHASES DR	ACCOUNTS PAYABLE DR	REF. NO.	BANK CR
		ACCOUNT	P.R.	AMOUNT					

 Name ______________ Date ______________

ANSWERS TO SECTION 12.2 EXERCISES (cont.)

Exercise 2, p. 433

1.
2.
3.
4.
5.
6.
7.
8.
9.
10.
11.
12.
13.
14.
15.
16.
17.
18.

Chapter 12

Name________________________ Date__________________

ANSWERS TO SECTION 12.2 EXERCISES (cont.)

Exercise 3, p. 433

SALES JOURNAL MONTH OF 19— Page

DATE		PARTICULARS	REF. NO.	ACCOUNTS RECEIVABLE DR	SALES CR	SALES TAX PAYABLE CR		

 Name ______________________ Date ________________

ANSWERS TO SECTION 12.2 EXERCISES (cont.)

Ex. 3 (cont.)

CASH RECEIPTS JOURNAL   MONTH OF   19—   Page

DATE	PARTICULARS	OTHER ACCOUNTS CR			SALES TAX PAYABLE CR	SALES CR	ACCOUNTS RECEIVABLE CR	REF. NO.	BANK CR
		ACCOUNT	P.R.	AMOUNT					

ANSWERS TO SECTION 12.2 EXERCISES (cont.)

Ex. 3 (cont.)

CASH PAYMENTS JOURNAL MONTH OF 19 — Page

DATE	PARTICULARS	OTHER ACCOUNTS DR			WAGES DR	SUPPLIES DR	ACCOUNTS PAYABLE DR	REF. NO.	BANK CR
		ACCOUNT	P.R.	AMOUNT					

ANSWERS TO SECTION 12.2 EXERCISES (cont.)

Ex. 3 (cont.)

PURCHASES JOURNAL MONTH OF 19— Page

DATE	PARTICULARS	OTHER ACCOUNTS DR			DELIVERY EXPENSE DR	SUPPLIES DR	PURCHASES DR	REF. NO.	ACCOUNTS PAYABLE CR
		ACCOUNT	P.R.	AMOUNT					

ANSWERS TO SECTION 12.2 EXERCISES (cont.)

Ex. 3 (cont.)

GENERAL JOURNAL

PAGE ____

DATE 19 —		PARTICULARS	P.R.	DEBIT	CREDIT

Exercise 4, p. 435 (Workbook Exercise)

Shown below for a merchandising business are the following:

- The five journals as at the end of a month in a very condensed form. The journals give the balanced figures needed for posting.
- The general ledger, in T-account form.

1. Post the five journals to the general ledger. Ignore dates and cross-referencing. Use checkmarks to indicate that postings have been completed.
2. Balance the general ledger.

CASH RECEIPTS JOURNAL

DATE		PARTICULARS	OTHER ACCOUNTS CR ACCOUNT	P.R.	AMOUNT	SALES TAX PAYABLE CR	SALES CR	ACCOUNTS RECEIVABLE CR	REF. NO.	BANK DR
		Refund	Purchases		50					
					50	82	1 640	1 670		3 442

 Name ______________ Date ______________

ANSWERS TO SECTION 12.2 EXERCISES (cont.)

Ex. 4 (cont.)

CASH PAYMENTS JOURNAL

DATE		PARTICULARS	OTHER ACCOUNTS DR			WAGES DR	PURCHASES DR	ACCOUNTS PAYABLE DR	REF. NO.	BA C
			ACCOUNT	P.R.	AMOUNT					
			Bank Charges		25					
			Supplies		75					
			Sales Tax Pyl		100					
			Rent		100					
			Telephone		20					
			Drawings		300					
					620	480	1 200	1 275		3

PURCHASES JOURNAL

DATE		PARTICULARS	OTHER ACCOUNTS DR			CAR EXPENSES DR	SUPPLIES DR	PURCHASES DR	REF. NO.	ACCO PAYA C
			ACCOUNT	P.R.	AMOUNT					
			Freight-in		15					
			General Ex.		50					
			Utilities Ex.		300					
					365	120	40	1 570		2

 Name________________ Date________________

ANSWERS TO SECTION 12.2 EXERCISES (cont.)

Ex. 4 (cont.)

SALES JOURNAL

DATE		PARTICULARS	REF. NO.		SALES TAX PAYABLE CR	SALES CR	ACCOUNTS RECEIVABLE DR
					92	1 840	1 932

GENERAL JOURNAL

DATE		PARTICULARS	P.R.	DR	CR
		General Expense		30	
		Supplies			30
		Correcting entry			

ANSWERS TO SECTION 12.2 EXERCISES (cont.)

Ex. 4 (cont.)

General Ledger

Bank	
3 140	

Accounts Receivable	
1 700	

Merchandise Inventory	
1 800	

Supplies	
200	

Equipment	
3 000	

Bank Loan	
	2 000

Accounts Payable	
	1 300

Sales Tax Payable	
	100

J.Webb Capital	
	4 040

J. Webb Drawings	
1 000	

Sales	
	12 500

Purchases	
4 000	

Freight-in	
200	

Bank Charges	
80	

Car Expenses	
1 000	

General Exp	
180	

Rent	
600	

ANSWERS TO SECTION 12.2 EXERCISES (cont.)

Ex. 4 (cont.)

General Ledger

Telephone	
100	

Utilities	
1 440	

Wages	
1500	

General Ledger Trial Balance

DRs.	CRs.

 Name________________ Date________________

ANSWERS TO SECTION 12.2 EXERCISES (cont.)

Exercise 5, p. 435 (Workbook Exercise)

C.D. Mould is the proprietor of Husky Hardware. He uses five journals and three ledgers in his accounting system. He posts the subsidiary ledgers daily, directly from the source documents. In his locality there is a 5 percent sales tax on all sales.

The three ledgers of Husky Hardware as of June 30, 19—, are set up for you.

The general ledger trial balance of Husky Hardware as of June 30, 19—, is as follows:

HUSKY HARDWARE
GENERAL LEDGER TRIAL BALANCE
JUNE 30, 19—

100	Bank	$26 142.00	
105	Accounts Receivable	4 125.00	
110	Merchandise Inventory	40 951.20	
115	Supplies	3 000.00	
120	Store Equipment	26 750.00	
125	Delivery Equipment	35 000.00	
200	Accounts Payable		$ 50 639.40
205	Sales Tax Payable		1 085.20
300	C.D. Mould, Capital		78 643.60
305	C.D. Mould, Drawings	58 763.40	
400	Sales		198 000.00
500	Purchases	95 000.00	
505	Miscellaneous Expense	2 164.10	
510	Rent	18 000.00	
515	Wages	18 472.50	
		$328 368.20	$328 368.20

The subsidiary ledger trial balances are as follows:

HUSKY HARDWARE
ACCOUNTS RECEIVABLE TRIAL BALANCE
JUNE 30, 19 —

J. Barkley, 260 Western Avenue	No. 490	$924.60	
	496	150.20	
	503	601.00	$1 675.80
T. Fairley, 300 Center Road	501		564.20
S. Harvey, 466 Keeley Street	502		765.00
R. Taylor, 588 Truway Drive	498		1 120.00
			$4 125.00

ANSWERS TO SECTION 12.2 EXERCISES (cont.)

Ex. 5 (cont.)

HUSKY HARDWARE
ACCOUNTS PAYABLE TRIAL BALANCE
JUNE 30, 19 —

Household Utensils Company 487 Faith Avenue	Inv. No. 52	$10 675.00
J. & A. Hardware Supply 600 Young Street	596	5 052.50
Learner Bros. 5012 Direct Avenue	141	30 672.00
Specialty Manufacturing Co. Barbary	163	4 239.90
		$50 639.40

1. **Journalize the transactions listed below in the five journals of Husky Hardware. These are provided for you.**

Cash Receipts Journal	*Page* 42
Cash Payments Journal	*Page* 93
Sales Journal	*Page* 56
Purchases Journal	*Page* 85
General Journal	*Page* 16

Transactions

July

2 *Cheque Copy*

— No. 187, to D. C. Harper, $3 000, for the rent for July.

Purchase Invoice

— From Household Utensils Company, No. 87, $1 845, for the purchase of merchandise.

3 *Sales Invoices*

— No. 504, to S. Harvey, $500 plus sales tax.

— No. 505, to R. Taylor, $260 plus sales tax.

— No. 506, to R. Fairley, $420 plus sales tax.

— No. 507, to J. Barkley, $640 plus sales tax.

4 *Cash Receipt*

— From the owner C. D. Mould, $10 000, for the purpose of increasing his investment in the business.

5 *Purchase Invoice*

— From Learner Brothers, No. 206, $356, for supplies.

Cheque Copy

— No. 188, to Supply House, $1 470, for the cash purchase of merchandise.

ANSWERS TO SECTION 12.2 EXERCISES (cont.)

Ex. 5 (cont.)

Cash Register Slips
— $8 632.05. The cash sales for the week amounted to $8 221 plus sales tax of $411.05.

8 *Cash Receipt*
— From T. Fairley, $564.20, paying invoice No. 501.

9 *Sales Invoices*
— No. 508, to L. Peck, 12 Semore St., $410 plus sales tax.
— No. 509, to S. Harvey, $180 plus sales tax.
— No. 510, to T. Fairley, $250 plus sales tax.

10 *Purchase Invoice*
— From J. & A. Hardware Supply, No. 612, $3 150, for a shipment of hammers, saws, and other tools.

12 *Cash Register Slips*
— $9 828. The cash sales for the week amounted to $9 360 plus sales tax of $468.
Bank Debt Memo
— From Sovereign Bank, $102, bank account decreased because of bank service charge.
Cheque Copy
— No. 189, to Modern Manufacturing Company, $2 730, for the cash purchase of merchandise.

13 *Cash Receipts*
— From S. Harvey, $1 290, paying invoices No. 502 and No. 504.
— From J. Barkley, $1 074.80 paying invoices No. 490 and No. 496.

15 *Cheque Copies*
— No. 190, to Learner Brothers, $15 000, on account.
— No. 191, to Household Utensils Company, $5 000, on account.
— No. 192, to B. Wiley, $1 250, wages for the first half of the month.
— No. 193, to W. Brown, $1 500, wages for the first half of the month.
— No. 194, to C. D. Mould, $2 000, personal withdrawal by proprietor.
— No. 195, to the Provincial Government, $1 085.20 sales tax for the previous month.

17 *Sales Invoices*
— No. 511, to V. Parker, 466 Janes Road, $750 plus sales tax.
— No. 512, to L. Peck, $450 plus sales tax.
— No. 513, to S. Harvey, $190 plus sales tax.
Cash Receipt
— From R. Taylor, $1120, paying invoice No. 498.

18 *Non-routine Transaction*
— The proprietor submits bills amounting to $240.80 for miscellaneous expenses which he has paid out of his own pocket. He asks that his Drawings account be credited.

ANSWERS TO SECTION 12.2 EXERCISES (cont.)

Ex. 5 (cont.)

19 *Cash Register Slips*
— $8 988. The cash sales for the week amounted to $8 560 plus $428 sales tax.
Cash Receipts
— From S. Harvey, $388.50 paying his account in full.
— From T. Fairley, $441.00 paying invoice No. 506.
— L. Peck, $430.50 paying invoice No. 508.

22 *Purchase Invoice*
— From Maple Feed Company, Maple, No. 996, $6 037.50, for the purchase of merchandise.

23 *Purchase Invoice*
— From Household Utensils Company, No. 156, $4 126.50 for the purchase of merchandise.

26 *Cash Register Slips*
— $11 182.50. The cash sales for the week amounted to $10 650 plus sales tax of $532.50.
Cheque Copy
— No. 196, to Learner Brothers, $2 625.00 for the cash purchase of merchandise.

29 *Cheque Copies*
— No. 197, to Household Utensils Company, $5 675, paying the balance of invoice No. 52.
— No. 198, to J. & A. Hardware Supply, $5 052.50 paying invoice No. 596.
— No. 199, to Specialty Manufacturing Company, $4 239.90 paying No. 163.

31 *Cheque Copies*
— No. 200, to B. Wiley, $1 250, wages for the last half of the month.
— No. 201, to W. Brown, $1 500, wages for the last half of the month.
— No. 202, to C. D. Mould, $800, for his personal use.

2. **Balance and post the journals to the general ledger.**
3. **Balance the general ledger.**
4. **Balance the subsidiary ledgers.**

 Name ______________________ Date ______________

ANSWERS TO SECTION 12.2 EXERCISES (cont.)

Ex. 5 (cont.)

SALES JOURNAL

PAGE 56

DATE		PARTICULARS	REF. NO.		SALES TAX PAYABLE CR	SALES CR	ACCOUNTS RECEIVABLE DR

GENERAL JOURNAL

PAGE 16

DATE		PARTICULARS	P.R.	DEBIT	CREDIT

WERS TO SECTION 12.2 EXERCISES (cont.)

(cont.)

DATE	PARTICULARS	ACCOUNT	P.R.	AMOUNT	PAYABLE CR	CR	RECEIVABLE CR	NO.	DR

PURCHASES JOURNAL

Page 85

DATE	PARTICULARS	OTHER ACCOUNTS DR ACCOUNT	P.R.	AMOUNT		SUPPLIES DR	PURCHASES DR	REF. NO.	ACCOUNTS PAYABLE CR

 Name ______________ Date ______________

ANSWERS TO SECTION 12.2 EXERCISES (cont.)

Ex. 5 (cont.)

CASH PAYMENTS JOURNAL

Page 93

DATE		PARTICULARS	OTHER ACCOUNTS DR			WAGES DR	ACCOUNTS PAYABLE DR	PURCHASES DR	REF. NO.	BANK CR
			ACCOUNT	P.R.	AMOUNT					

Name ____________________ Date ______________

ANSWERS TO SECTION 12.2 EXERCISES (cont.)

Ex. 5 (cont.)

GENERAL LEDGER

ACCOUNT Bank **NO.** 100

DATE 19—		PARTICULARS	P.R.	DEBIT	CREDIT	D/C	BALANCE
June	30	Balance Forward	—			D	26 142 –

ACCOUNT Accounts Receivable **NO.** 105

DATE 19—		PARTICULARS	P.R.	DEBIT	CREDIT	D/C	BALANCE
June	30	Balance Forward	—			D	4 125 –

ACCOUNT Merchandise Inventory **NO.** 110

DATE 19—		PARTICULARS	P.R.	DEBIT	CREDIT	D/C	BALANCE
June	30	Balance Forward	—			D	40 951 20

ACCOUNT Supplies **NO.** 115

DATE 19—		PARTICULARS	P.R.	DEBIT	CREDIT	D/C	BALANCE
June	30	Balance Forward	—			D	3 000 –

ACCOUNT Store Equipment **NO.** 120

DATE 19—		PARTICULARS	P.R.	DEBIT	CREDIT	D/C	BALANCE
June	30	Balance Forward	—			D	26 750 –

ACCOUNT Delivery Equipment **NO.** 125

DATE 19—		PARTICULARS	P.R.	DEBIT	CREDIT	D/C	BALANCE
June	30	Balance Forward	—			D	35 000 –

 Name________________ Date________________

ANSWERS TO SECTION 12.2 EXERCISES (cont.)

Ex. 5 (cont.)

ACCOUNT Accounts Payable **NO.** 200

DATE 19—		PARTICULARS	P.R.	DEBIT	CREDIT	D/C	BALANCE
June	30	Balance Forward	—			C	50 639 40

ACCOUNT Sales Tax Payable **NO.** 205

DATE 19—		PARTICULARS	P.R.	DEBIT	CREDIT	D/C	BALANCE
June	30	Balance Forward	—			C	1 085 20

ACCOUNT C.D. Mould, Capital **NO.** 300

DATE 19—		PARTICULARS	P.R.	DEBIT	CREDIT	D/C	BALANCE
June	30	Balance Forward	—			C	78 643 60

ACCOUNT C.D. Mould, Drawings **NO.** 305

DATE 19—		PARTICULARS	P.R.	DEBIT	CREDIT	D/C	BALANCE
June	30	Balance Forward	—			D	58 763 40

ACCOUNT Sales **NO.** 400

DATE 19—		PARTICULARS	P.R.	DEBIT	CREDIT	D/C	BALANCE
June	30	Balance Forward	—			C	198 000 –

 Name____________________ Date______________

ANSWERS TO SECTION 12.2 EXERCISES (cont.)

Ex. 5 (cont.)

ACCOUNT Purchases **NO.** 500

DATE 19—		PARTICULARS	P.R.	DEBIT	CREDIT	D/C	BALANCE
June	30	Balance Forward	—			D	95 000 –

ACCOUNT Miscellaneous Expense **NO.** 505

DATE 19—		PARTICULARS	P.R.	DEBIT	CREDIT	D/C	BALANCE
June	30	Balance Forward	—			D	2 164 10

ACCOUNT Rent **NO.** 510

DATE 19—		PARTICULARS	P.R.	DEBIT	CREDIT	D/C	BALANCE
June	30	Balance Forward	—			D	18 000 –

ACCOUNT Wages **NO.** 515

DATE 19—		PARTICULARS	P.R.	DEBIT	CREDIT	D/C	BALANCE
June	30	Balance Forward	—			D	18 472 50

 Name ______ Date ______

ANSWERS TO SECTION 12.2 EXERCISES (cont.)

Ex. 5 (cont.)

ACCOUNTS RECEIVABLE LEDGER

ACCOUNT J. Barkley, 260 Western Avenue **NO.**

DATE 19—		PARTICULARS	P.R.	DEBIT	CREDIT	D/C	BALANCE
June	30	Inv. 490 – 924.60	—				
	30	496 – 150.20	—				
	30	503 – 601.00	—			D	1675 80

ACCOUNT T. Fairley, 300 Center Road **NO.**

DATE 19—		PARTICULARS	P.R.	DEBIT	CREDIT	D/C	BALANCE
June	30	Inv. 501	—			D	564 20

ACCOUNT S. Harvey, 466 Keeley Street **NO.**

DATE 19—		PARTICULARS	P.R.	DEBIT	CREDIT	D/C	BALANCE
June	30	Inv. 502	—			D	765 –

ACCOUNT V. Parker, 466 Janes Road **NO.**

DATE 19—		PARTICULARS	P.R.	DEBIT	CREDIT	D/C	BALANCE

ANSWERS TO SECTION 12.2 EXERCISES (cont.)

Ex. 5 (cont.)

ACCOUNT L. Peck, 12 Semore St. **NO.**

DATE 19—		PARTICULARS	P.R.	DEBIT	CREDIT	D/C	BALANCE

ACCOUNT R. Taylor, 588 Truway Drive **NO.**

DATE 19—		PARTICULARS	P.R.	DEBIT	CREDIT	D/C	BALANCE
June	30	Inv. 498				D	1120 –

ACCOUNTS PAYABLE LEDGER

ACCOUNT Household Utensils Company, 487 Faith Avenue **NO.**

DATE 19—		PARTICULARS	P.R.	DEBIT	CREDIT	D/C	BALANCE
June	30	Purch. Inv. #52	—			C	10675 –

ACCOUNT J. & A. Hardware Supply, 600 Young Street **NO.**

DATE 19—		PARTICULARS	P.R.	DEBIT	CREDIT	D/C	BALANCE
June	30	Purch. Inv. #596	—			C	5052 50

 Name______________ Date______________

ANSWERS TO SECTION 12.2 EXERCISES (cont.)

Ex. 5 (cont.)

ACCOUNT Learner Bros., 5012 Direct Avenue **NO.**

DATE 19—		PARTICULARS	P.R.	DEBIT	CREDIT	D/C	BALANCE
June	30	Purch. Inv. #141	—			C	30 672 –

ACCOUNT Maple Feed Company, Maple **NO.**

DATE 19—		PARTICULARS	P.R.	DEBIT	CREDIT	D/C	BALANCE

ACCOUNT Specialty Manufacturing Co., Barbary **NO.**

DATE 19—		PARTICULARS	P.R.	DEBIT	CREDIT	D/C	BALANCE
June	30	Purch. Inv. #163	—			C	4 239 90

 Name______________ Date______________

ANSWERS TO SECTION 12.2 EXERCISES (cont.)

Ex. 5 (cont.)

Name ______________________ Date ______________

ANSWERS TO SECTION 12.2 EXERCISES (cont.)

Ex. 5 (cont.)

Chapter 12

Name____________________ Date________________

ANSWERS TO SECTION 12.3 REVIEW QUESTIONS (text, p. 441)

Cash Discounts

1. ____

2. ____

3. ____

4. ____

5. ____

6. ____

7. ____

8. ____

9. ____

10. ____

11. ____

12. ____

13. ____

14. ____

15. ____

16. ____

ANSWERS TO SECTION 12.3 EXERCISES (text, p. 441)

Exercise 1, p. 441

DATE OF INVOICE	AMOUNT OF INVOICE	TERMS OF SALE	AMOUNT OF CREDIT NOTE	DATE OF CREDIT NOTE	DATE PAYMENT IS MADE	AMOUNT OF PAYMENT REQUIRED
Mar. 12	$52.50	2/10, N/30	—	—	Mar. 20	
May 18	47.25	Net 30	—	—	May 27	
Sept. 4	115.50	3/15, N/60	—	—	Oct. 10	
Feb. 6	1 050.00	1/20, N/60	$126.00	Feb. 18	Mar. 6	
Oct. 19	588.00	2/10, N/30	42.00	Nov. 5	Nov. 27	
Aug. 27	882.00	2/15, N/60	168.00	Sept. 7	Sept. 10	

ANSWERS TO SECTION 12.3 EXERCISES (cont.)

Exercise 2, p. 442

DATE OF INVOICE	INVOICE AMOUNT	TERMS OF SALE	AMOUNT OF CREDIT NOTE	DATE OF CREDIT NOTE	DATE PAYMENT IS REQUIRED	AMOUNT OF PAYMENT REQUIRED
May 14	$147.00	2/10, N/30	—	—		
Apr. 15	315.00	3/20, N/60	$42.00	May 1		
June. 3	220.05	2/10, N/60	78.75	Jun. 20		
Nov. 20	59.25	2/15, N/60	36.75	Dec. 2		

Exercise 3, p. 442

GENERAL JOURNAL

PAGE ______

	DATE	PARTICULARS	P.R.	DEBIT	CREDIT
		IN THE BOOKS OF CIRCLE SUPPLY			
1. a.					
1. b.					
		IN THE BOOKS OF WATSON CONSTRUCTION			
2. a.					
2. b.					

ANSWERS TO SECTION 12.3 EXERCISES (cont.)

Exercise 4, p. 443

GENERAL JOURNAL PAGE ______

DATE		PARTICULARS	P.R.	DEBIT	CREDIT
IN THE BOOKS OF CIRCLE SUPPLY					
IN THE BOOKS OF JACKSON AND JACKSON					

 Name__________ Date__________

ANSWERS TO COMPUTER REVIEW 12.4 QUESTIONS (text, p. 449)

Using Bedford in the Accounting Cycle

1.

2.

3.

4.

5.

COMMUNICATE IT

 Name________________________ Date__________________

ANSWERS TO CHAPTER 12 EXERCISES (text, p. 450)

USING YOUR KNOWLEDGE

Exercise 1, p. 450

Indicate whether each of the following statements is true or false by placing a "T" or an "F" in the space indicated. Explain the reason for each "F" response in the space provided.

1. The general journal is not normally used if the business has a synoptic journal. ☐
2. There is a special column for every general ledger account in the synoptic journal. ☐
3. The chief disadvantage of the synoptic journal is that you have to post column totals. ☐
4. An accounting entry that takes more than one line cannot be recorded in the synoptic journal. ☐
5. There would be a special column for Rent Expense in the synoptic journal. ☐
6. The synoptic journal is balanced at the end of every page. ☐
7. The date used when formally posting the synoptic journal is the last day of the month. ☐
8. A credit to Sales in the synoptic journal would normally be entered in the Other Accounts Credit column. ☐
9. All sales of merchandise are recorded in the sales journal. ☐
10. The cash payments journal is also known as the cash disbursements journal. ☐
11. Additional cash invested in the business by the owner would be recorded in the general journal. ☐
12. A bank debit advice requires an entry in the cash receipts journal. ☐
13. The five journal system inevitably leads to the clerks becoming specialists within the system. ☐
14. The general ledger would not balance if only four of the five journals were posted. ☐
15. A purchase partly for cash and partly on account would be recorded in the purchases journal. ☐

Explanations

____

____

____

____

____

ANSWERS TO CHAPTER 12 EXERCISES (cont.)

Ex. 1 (cont.)

Exercise 2, p. 451

1. As a result of the two offsetting errors:

2.

Exercise 3, p. 451

1.

2.

Exercise 4, p. 451

Exercise 5, p. 451

a.

b.

 Name________________ Date________

ANSWERS TO CHAPTER 12 EXERCISES (cont.)

Exercise 6, p. 452

The advantages are:

The disadvantages are:

Exercise 7, p. 452

Exercise 8, p. 452

1.

2.

3.

4.

5.

 Name________________ Date________

ANSWERS TO CHAPTER 12 EXERCISES (cont.)

Exercise 9, p. 452

GENERAL JOURNAL

PAGE ______

DATE		PARTICULARS	P.R.	DEBIT	CREDIT
IN THE BOOKS OF CIRCLE SUPPLY					
1.					
IN THE BOOKS OF KITCHEN CABINETRY					
2.					

 Name ______________ Date ______________

ANSWERS TO CHAPTER 12 EXERCISES (cont.)

Exercise 10, p. 454

ANSWERS TO CHAPTER 12 EXERCISES (cont.)

COMPREHENSIVE EXERCISES

Exercise 11, p. 455 (Workbook Exercise)

The general ledger of Bristol Appliances Company as of December 31, 19 — is set up below. On December 31, 19 — the combined chart of accounts and general ledger trial balance is as follows:

No.	Account	DR	CR
105	Bank	$ 6 163.12	
110	Accounts Receivable	12 471.49	
115	Supplies	312.50	
120	Merchandise Inventory	17 416.40	
125	Store Equipment	3 800.00	
130	Delivery Equipment	22 200.00	
205	Accounts Payable		$11 941.60
210	Bank Loan		8 000.00
215	Sales Tax Payable		360.00
305	S.C. Scales, Capital		42 061.91
310	S.C. Scales, Drawings		
405	Sales		
505	Purchases		
510	Delivery Expense		
515	General Expense		
520	Rent		
525	Salaries		
		$ 62 363.51	$ 62 363.51

The subsidiary ledgers of Bristol Appliances Company as of December 31, 19 — are set up below. On December 31, 19 —, the subsidiary trial balances appeared as follows:

ACCOUNTS RECEIVABLE TRIAL BALANCE
DECEMBER 31, 19 —

C. Bruk	Inv. No. 325	$ 316.10
M. Howard	296	3 095.00
J. Joss	306	912.75
O. Langley	315	163.87
T. Miles	326	5 050.00
S. Pampu	217	135.00
D. Wilkins	331	2 798.77
		$ 12 471.49

ANSWERS TO CHAPTER 12 EXERCISES (cont.)

Ex. 11 (cont.)

ACCOUNTS PAYABLE TRIAL BALANCE

DECEMBER 31, 19 —

Stirling Company, 20 River Street	Ref. B245	$ 4 560.20
Triangle Electric, Roxborough	4701	4 316.47
Universal Vacuums, 20 Dexter Street	6508	1 000.00
Western Electric, 1000 Fleet Street	246R	2 064.93
		$ 11 941.60

The subsidiary ledgers of Bristol Appliances Company are posted daily, directly from the source documents.

1. **In the journals of Bristol Appliances Company, record the transactions shown below. Bristol Appliances uses a five-journal system. The five journals shown below are set up in the workbook. Use the following page numbers.**

Cash Receipts Journal	*Page* 61
Cash Payments Journal	*Page* 117
Purchases Journal	*Page* 74
Sales Journal	*Page* 82
General Journal	*Page* 29

A five per cent sales tax is to be applied on all sales of merchandise.

Transactions

January

2 *Cash Sales Slip*

— No. 401, to T. Arthur, $125 plus sales tax.

Cash Receipt

— From C. Bruk, $116.10, on account.

Cheque Copy

— No. 376, to J.C. Brown, $87.42, for the cash purchase of supplies.

3 *Purchase Invoice*

— No. 1212, from Smith's Service Station, 3 Cary Street, $263.50 for gasoline and oil used in the delivery truck.

Cash Sales Slip

— No. 402, to R. Malone, $475 plus sales tax.

4 *Sales Invoice*

— No. 347, to M. Howard, $310 plus sales tax.

5 *Cheque Copies*

— No. 377, to Universal Vacuums, $500, on account.

— No. 378, to "Cash," $885, for the salaries for the week.

8 *Cash Receipt*

— From T. Miles, $5 050.00 in full payment of account.

Correcting Entry

— An error was discovered in an entry made in December. An amount of $16.10 was debited incorrectly to Delivery Expense; it should have been debited to General Expense.

9 *Cash Sales Slip*

— No. 403, to H. McPhee, $800 plus sales tax.

ANSWERS TO CHAPTER 12 EXERCISES (cont.)

Ex. 11 (cont.)

10 *Purchase Invoice*
— No. 306R, from Western Electric, $661.50, for the purchase of merchandise.
Cheque Copy
— No. 379, to Stirling Company, $708.75, for the cash purchase of merchandise.

11 *Sales Invoices*
— No. 348, to O. Langley, $137.50 plus sales tax.
— No. 349, to T. Miles, $200 plus sales tax.
— No. 350, to S. Pampu, $475.12 plus sales tax.

12 *Cash Receipt*
— From Clover Stores, $105; because of a recent change in the system, certain supplies on hand were not usable and were sold for cash at their cost of $105.
Cheque Copy
— No. 380, to "Cash," $710, for the salaries for the week.

15 *Cheque Copies*
— No. 381, to S.C. Scales, $300, for his personal use.
— No. 382, to the Provincial Government, $360, for sales tax for the previous month.
Cash Receipts
— From C. Bruk, $100, on account.
— From J. Joss, $512.75, on account.
— From S. Pampu, $135, paying invoice No. 217.
— From D. Wilkins, $2 798.77, paying invoices No. 331 and 346.
Cash Sales Slips
— No. 404, to F. Lang, $480 plus sales tax.
— No. 405, to K. Klein, $750 plus sales tax.

16 *Purchase Invoice*
— No. 406, from Ritz Furniture, Melody Road, $1157.50 for the purchase of merchandise.

17 *Purchase Invoice*
— No. 708, from Super Stationers, $76.40, for supplies.

18 *Cheque Copies*
— No. 383, to Triangle Electric, $4 316.47, paying invoice No. 4701.
— No. 384, to Stirling Company, $4 560.20, paying invoice No. B245.
— No. 385, to Western Electric, $2 064.93, paying invoice no. 246R.
— No. 386, to Smith's Service Station, $263.50, paying invoice No. 1212.

19 *Cheque Copy*
— No. 387, to "Cash," $890, in payment of the weekly salaries.

22 *Sales Invoices*
— No. 351, to D. Wilkins, $300 plus sales tax.
— No. 352, to C. Bruk, $281.63 plus sales tax.
— No. 353, to S. Pampu, $31.12 plus sales tax.

23 *Purchase Invoice*
— No. 4912, from Triangle Electric, $968.00, for purchase of merchandise.

24 *Purchase Invoice*
— No. 842, from Super Stationers, $251.75, for supplies.

25 *Cheque Copy*
— No. 388, to local telephone company, $46.50, for monthly telephone bill.

ANSWERS TO CHAPTER 12 EXERCISES (cont.)

Ex. 11 (cont.)

26 *Cheque Copies*
— No. 389, to Boston Television Co., $412.60, for the cash purchase of merchandise.
— No. 390, to Admirable Company, $592.95, for the cash purchase of merchandise.
— No. 391, to "Cash," $875, for the weekly salaries.
— No. 392, to Grayson Brothers, $450, for the rent for the month.

30 *Purchase Invoice*
— No. 864, from Super Stationers, $105, for supplies.

31 *Purchase Invoices*
— No. B319, from Stirling Company, $315, for merchandise.
— No. 6722, from Universal Vacuums, $261.81, for merchandise.
— No. 512, from Ritz Furniture, $640.70 for merchandise.

Cash Sales Slip
— No. 406, to M. Morse, $906.00 plus sales tax.

Sales Invoices
— No. 354, to J. Joss, $1 200 plus sales tax.
— No. 355, M. Howard, $12.08 plus sales tax.
— No. 356, to S. Pampu, $19.65 plus sales tax.

Cheque Copy
— No. 393, to local hydro, $96.40, for hydro for the month.

2. **Balance the special journals and post the five journals to the general ledger.**
3. **Balance the general ledger as of January 31.**
4. **Balance the subsidiary ledgers as of January 31.**

 Name ____________________ Date ______________

ANSWERS TO CHAPTER 12 EXERCISES (cont.)

Ex. 11 (cont.)

CASH RECEIPTS JOURNAL

Page 61

DATE	PARTICULARS	OTHER ACCOUNTS DR			ACCOUNTS RECEIVABLE CR	SALES TAX PAYABLE CR	SALES CR	REF. NO.	BANK DR
		ACCOUNT	P.R.	AMOUNT					

ANSWERS TO CHAPTER 12 EXERCISES (cont.)

Ex. 11 (cont.)

CASH PAYMENTS JOURNAL **Page 117**

DATE	PARTICULARS	OTHER ACCOUNTS DR			ACCOUNTS PAYABLE DR	SALARIES DR	PURCHASES DR	REF. NO.	BANK CR
		ACCOUNT	P.R.	AMOUNT					

 Name ________________ Date ____________

ANSWERS TO CHAPTER 12 EXERCISES (cont.)

Ex. 11 (cont.)

SALES JOURNAL Page 82

DATE		PARTICULARS	OTHER ACCOUNTS CR				SALES TAX PAYABLE CR	SALES CR	REF. NO.	ACCOUNTS RECEIVABLE DR
			ACCOUNT	P.R.	AMOUNT					

ANSWERS TO CHAPTER 12 EXERCISES (cont.)

Ex. 11 (cont.)

PURCHASES JOURNAL Page 74

DATE		PARTICULARS	OTHER ACCOUNTS DR			DELIVERY EXPENSE DR	SUPPLIES DR	PURCHASES DR	REF. NO.	ACCOUNTS PAYABLE CR
			ACCOUNT	P.R.	AMOUNT					

ANSWERS TO CHAPTER 12 EXERCISES (cont.)

Ex. 11 (cont.)

GENERAL JOURNAL

PAGE 29

DATE 19—		PARTICULARS	P.R.	DEBIT	CREDIT

GENERAL LEDGER

ACCOUNT Bank NO. 105

DATE 19—		PARTICULARS	P.R.	DEBIT	CREDIT	D/C	BALANCE
Dec.	31	Forwarded	—			D	6 163 12

ACCOUNT Accounts Receivable NO. 110

DATE 19—		PARTICULARS	P.R.	DEBIT	CREDIT	D/C	BALANCE
Dec.	31	Forwarded	—			D	12 471 49

ANSWERS TO CHAPTER 12 EXERCISES (cont.)

Ex. 11 (cont.)

ACCOUNT Supplies NO. 115

DATE 19—		PARTICULARS	P.R.	DEBIT	CREDIT	D/C	BALANCE
Dec.	31	Forwarded	—			D	312.50

ACCOUNT Merchandise Inventory NO. 120

DATE 19—		PARTICULARS	P.R.	DEBIT	CREDIT	D/C	BALANCE
Dec.	31	Forwarded	—			D	17,416.40

ACCOUNT Store Equipment NO. 125

DATE 19—		PARTICULARS	P.R.	DEBIT	CREDIT	D/C	BALANCE
Dec.	31	Forwarded	—			D	3,800.–

ACCOUNT Delivery Equipment NO. 130

DATE 19—		PARTICULARS	P.R.	DEBIT	CREDIT	D/C	BALANCE
Dec.	30	Forwarded	—			D	22,200.–

ANSWERS TO CHAPTER 12 EXERCISES (cont.)

Ex. 11 (cont.)

ACCOUNT Accounts Payable **NO.** 205

DATE 19—		PARTICULARS	P.R.	DEBIT	CREDIT	D/C	BALANCE
Dec.	31	Forwarded	—			C	11 941 60

ACCOUNT Bank Loan **NO.** 210

DATE 19—		PARTICULARS	P.R.	DEBIT	CREDIT	D/C	BALANCE
Dec.	31	Forwarded	—			C	8 000 –

ACCOUNT Sales Tax Payable **NO.** 215

DATE 19—		PARTICULARS	P.R.	DEBIT	CREDIT	D/C	BALANCE
Dec.	31	Forwarded	—			C	360 –

ANSWERS TO CHAPTER 12 EXERCISES (cont.)

Ex. 11 (cont.)

ACCOUNT S.C. Scales, Capital **NO.** 305

DATE 19—		PARTICULARS	P.R.	DEBIT	CREDIT	D/C	BALANCE
Dec.	31	Forwarded	—			C	42 061 91

ACCOUNT S.C. Scales, Drawings **NO.** 310

DATE 19—		PARTICULARS	P.R.	DEBIT	CREDIT	D/C	BALANCE

ACCOUNT Sales **NO.** 405

DATE 19—		PARTICULARS	P.R.	DEBIT	CREDIT	D/C	BALANCE

ACCOUNT Purchases **NO.** 505

DATE 19—		PARTICULARS	P.R.	DEBIT	CREDIT	D/C	BALANCE

ACCOUNT Delivery Expense **NO.** 510

DATE 19—		PARTICULARS	P.R.	DEBIT	CREDIT	D/C	BALANCE

 Name ______________ Date ______________

ANSWERS TO CHAPTER 12 EXERCISES (cont.)

Ex. 11 (cont.)

ACCOUNT General Expense NO. 515

DATE 19—		PARTICULARS	P.R.	DEBIT	CREDIT	D/C	BALANCE

ACCOUNT Rent NO. 520

DATE 19—		PARTICULARS	P.R.	DEBIT	CREDIT	D/C	BALANCE

ACCOUNT Salaries NO. 525

DATE 19—		PARTICULARS	P.R.	DEBIT	CREDIT	D/C	BALANCE

ACCOUNTS RECEIVABLE LEDGER

ACCOUNT C. Bruk NO.

DATE 19—		PARTICULARS	P.R.	DEBIT	CREDIT	D/C	BALANCE
Dec.	31	Forwarded # 325	—			D	3 1 6 10

 Name ____________ Date ____________

ANSWERS TO CHAPTER 12 EXERCISES (cont.)

Ex. 11 (cont.)

ACCOUNT M. Howard NO.

DATE 19—		PARTICULARS	P.R.	DEBIT	CREDIT	D/C	BALANCE
Dec.	31	Forwarded #296	—			D	3095 –

ACCOUNT J. Joss NO.

DATE 19—		PARTICULARS	P.R.	DEBIT	CREDIT	D/C	BALANCE
Dec.	31	Forwarded # 306	—			D	912 75

ACCOUNT O. Langley NO.

DATE 19—		PARTICULARS	P.R.	DEBIT	CREDIT	D/C	BALANCE
Dec.	30	Forwarded # 315	—			D	163 87

ACCOUNT T. Miles NO.

DATE 19—		PARTICULARS	P.R.	DEBIT	CREDIT	D/C	BALANCE
Dec.	31	Forwarded # 326	—			D	5050 –

ANSWERS TO CHAPTER 12 EXERCISES (cont.)

Ex. 11 (cont.)

ACCOUNT S. Pampu **NO.**

DATE 19—		PARTICULARS	P.R.	DEBIT	CREDIT	D/C	BALANCE
Dec.	31	Forwarded # 217	—			D	135 –

ACCOUNT D. Wilkins **NO.**

DATE 19—		PARTICULARS	P.R.	DEBIT	CREDIT	D/C	BALANCE
Dec.	31	Forwarded #331 2500. – #346 298.77				D	2798 77

ACCOUNTS PAYABLE LEDGER

ACCOUNT Ritz Furniture **NO.**

DATE 19—		PARTICULARS	P.R.	DEBIT	CREDIT	D/C	BALANCE

ACCOUNT Smith's Service Station **NO.**

DATE 19—		PARTICULARS	P.R.	DEBIT	CREDIT	D/C	BALANCE

ANSWERS TO CHAPTER 12 EXERCISES (cont.)

Ex. 11 (cont.)

ACCOUNT Stirling Company NO.

DATE 19—		PARTICULARS	P.R.	DEBIT	CREDIT	D/C	BALANCE
Dec.	31	Forwarded # B245	—			C	4 5 6 0 20

ACCOUNT Super Stationers NO.

DATE 19—		PARTICULARS	P.R.	DEBIT	CREDIT	D/C	BALANCE

ACCOUNT Triangle Electric NO.

DATE 19—		PARTICULARS	P.R.	DEBIT	CREDIT	D/C	BALANCE
Dec.	31	Forwarded # 4701	—			C	4 3 1 6 47

ACCOUNT Universal Vacuums NO.

DATE 19—		PARTICULARS	P.R.	DEBIT	CREDIT	D/C	BALANCE
Dec.	31	Forwarded # 6508	—			C	1 0 0 0 –

ACCOUNT Western Electric NO.

DATE 19—		PARTICULARS	P.R.	DEBIT	CREDIT	D/C	BALANCE
Dec.	31	Forwarded # 246R	—			C	2 0 6 4 93

 Name ______________________ Date ______________

ANSWERS TO CHAPTER 12 EXERCISES (cont.)

Ex. 11 (cont.)

____

____

____

GENERAL LEDGER TRIAL BALANCE, JANUARY 31

ANSWERS TO CHAPTER 12 EXERCISES (cont.)

Ex. 11 (cont.)

ACCOUNTS RECEIVABLE LEDGER, JANUARY 31, 19 —

ACCOUNTS PAYABLE LEDGER, JANUARY 31, 19 —

ANSWERS TO CHAPTER 12 EXERCISES (cont.)

Exercise 12, p. 455 (Workbook Exercise)

The accountant for Midwest Supply has just posted the five journals and taken off a trial balance at the end of April. The five journals, general ledger, and trial balance are shown below, in simplified form. As you can see, the trial balance does not balance.
Locate and correct the error or errors and prepare a corrected trial balance.

CASH PAYMENTS JOURNAL

DATE		PARTICULARS	OTHER ACCOUNTS			WAGES DR	PURCHASES DR	ACCOUNTS PAYABLE DR	REF. NO.	BANK CR
			ACCOUNT	P.R.	AMOUNT					
Apr	2	P. Agnew						350		350
	3	T. Borgo				70				70
	4	R. Tait	Supplies	✔	40					40
	9	R. Strom					110			110
	10	Prov. Treas.	Sales Tax Py'l	✔	150					150
	12	P. Olenik						500		500
	17	J. Klak	Drawings	✔	120					120
	18	C. Over				60				60
	23	J. Erasmus	Rent	✔	75					75
	24	V. Star					100			100
	29	Dom Bank	Bank Chgs	✔	5					5
	30	A. Martin				70				70
					390	200	210	850		1 650
						✔	✔	✔		✔

ANSWERS TO CHAPTER 12 EXERCISES (cont.)

Ex. 12 (cont.)

CASH RECEIPTS JOURNAL

DATE		PARTICULARS	OTHER ACCOUNTS CR			SALES TAX PAYABLE CR	SALES CR	ACCOUNTS RECEIVABLE CR	REF. NO.	BANK DR
			ACCOUNT	P.R.	AMOUNT					
Apr	1	D. Moore						200		200
	5	K. Iwasa				14	140			154
	8	C. Iven						150		150
	10	G. Miele				2	20			22
	12	R. Paradis						300		300
	22	N. Opie				12	120			132
	24	G. Orr						400		400
	26	Dom Bk	Bank Chgs	✔	30					30
	26	C. Pogue						180		180
	29	R. Sax				10	100			110
	29	D. Takala						90		90
	30	F. Tam						285		285
					30	38	380	1 605		2 053
						✔	✔	✔		✔

ANSWERS TO CHAPTER 12 EXERCISES (cont.)

Ex. 12 (cont.)

PURCHASES JOURNAL

DATE		PARTICULARS	OTHER ACCOUNTS DR			CAR EXPENSE DR	SUPPLIES DR	PURCHASES DR	REF. NO.	ACCOUNTS PAYABLE CR
			ACCOUNT	P.R.	AMOUNT					
Apr	2	Superior Pr.						180		180
	3	Brucker's					50			50
	5	Lawrence Bros.	Freight-in	✓	105					105
	9	Kam Motors				120				120
	10	Astra Supply						330		330
	11	City Hydro	Utilities	✓	150					150
	16	Tidy Service						240		240
	19	Iron Work	Gen'l Exp	✓	80					80
	26	Lawin's					40			40
	29	Dom. Motors				120				120
					335	240	90	750		1 415
						✓	✓	✓		✓

ANSWERS TO CHAPTER 12 EXERCISES (cont.)

Ex. 12 (cont.)

SALES JOURNAL

DATE		PARTICULARS	REF. NO.		SALES TAX PAYABLE CR	SALES CR	ACCOUNTS RECEIVABLE DR
Apr.	1	P. Kay	16		11	110	121
	4	R. Greco	17		12	120	132
	5	C. Demian	18		7	70	77
	8	J. Azak	19		20	200	220
	11	N. Poirier	20		10	100	110
	15	A. McComb	21		8	80	88
	15	T. Hunt	22		4	40	44
	16	S. Wilson	23		21	210	231
	19	B. Tardif	24		15	150	165
	22	S. Squire	25		13	130	143
	25	O. Park	26		7	70	77
	26	C. McDaid	27		6	60	66
	30	Y. Chin	28		11	110	121
					145	1 450	1 595
					✔	✔	✔

GENERAL JOURNAL

DATE		PARTICULARS	P.R.	DR	CR
Apr.	8	General Expense	✔	35	
		Utilities	✔		35
	29	Freight-in	✔	12	
		Car Expense	✔		12

ANSWERS TO CHAPTER 12 EXERCISES (cont.)

Ex. 12 (cont.)

GENERAL LEDGER

Bank

Dr	Cr
150	***1 605***
2 053	
(***598***)	

Accounts Rec'l

Dr	Cr
2 400	***1 605***
1 595	
(***2 390***)	

Loan Receivable

Dr	Cr
1 000	
(***1 000***)	

Mdse Inventory

Dr	Cr
1 200	
(***1 200***)	

Supplies

Dr	Cr
170	
40	
90	
(***290***)	

Equipment

Dr	Cr
2 150	
(***2 150***)	

Bank Loan

Dr	Cr
	675
	(***675***)

Accounts Pay'l

Dr	Cr
805	890
	1541
	(***1 626***)

Sales Tax Pay'l

Dr	Cr
150	150
	38
	145
	(***183***)

J. Klak Capital

Dr	Cr
	7 527
	(***7 527***)

J. Klak Drawings

Dr	Cr
875	
120	
(***995***)	

Sales

Dr	Cr
	5 200
	380
	1 450
	(***7 030***)

Purchases

Dr	Cr
2 750	
210	
750	
(***3 710***)	

Freight-in

Dr	Cr
212	
105	
12	
(***329***)	

Bank Charges

Dr	Cr
50	
5	
30	
(***85***)	

Car Expenses

Dr	Cr
720	***12***
240	
(***948***)	

General Exp

Dr	Cr
390	
80	
35	
(***505***)	

Rent

Dr	Cr
375	
75	
(***450***)	

ANSWERS TO CHAPTER 12 EXERCISES (cont.)

Ex. 12 (cont.)

Utilities	
850	
150	
35	
(1 035)	

Wages	
1 150	
200	
(1 350)	

TRIAL BALANCE

DR	CR
598	675
2 390	1 626
1 000	183
1 200	7 527
290	7 030
2 150	
995	
3 710	
329	
85	
948	
505	
450	
1 035	
1 350	
17 035	17 041

Name ____________________ Date ________________

ANSWERS TO CHAPTER 12 EXERCISES (cont.)

Challenge Exercise

Exercise 13, p. 455

GENERAL JOURNAL PAGE *124*

DATE 19—		PARTICULARS	P.R.	DEBIT	CREDIT

ANSWERS TO CHAPTER 12 EXERCISES (cont.)

Ex. 13 (cont.)

GENERAL JOURNAL

PAGE 125

DATE 19 —		PARTICULARS	P.R.	DEBIT	CREDIT

 Name______________ Date______________

ANSWERS TO CHAPTER 12 EXERCISES (cont.)

Ex. 13 (cont.)

GENERAL JOURNAL

PAGE 126

DATE 19—		PARTICULARS	P.R.	DEBIT	CREDIT

ANSWERS TO CHAPTER 12 EXERCISES (cont.)

Ex. 13 (cont.)

GENERAL JOURNAL

PAGE 127

DATE 19—		PARTICULARS	P.R.	DEBIT	CREDIT

 Name________________ Date________________

ANSWERS TO CHAPTER 12 EXERCISES (cont.)

FOR FURTHER THOUGHT

Exercise 14, p. 456

1. ____

2. ____

3. ____

4. ____

5. ____

6. ____

7. ____

8. ____

9. ____

10. ____

11. ____

12. ____

13. ____

14. ____

15. ____

ANSWERS TO CHAPTER 12 EXERCISES (cont.)

Ex. 14 (cont.)

16. ______________________

17. ______________________

18. a. ______________________

b. ______________________

c. ______________________

d. ______________________

e. ______________________

CASE STUDIES (text, p. 458)

Case 1 *No Journal!*, p. 458

1. ______________________

2. ______________________

3. ______________________

4. ______________________

5. ______________________

6. ______________________

 Name ______________ Date ______________

CASE STUDIES (cont.)

Case 2 *Squeeze Play*, p. 460

1.

2.

3.

4.

Case 3 *Crook or Saint?*, p. 460

1.

2.

 Name______________ Date______________

CASE STUDIES (cont.)

3. ______________________________
____
____

4. ______________________________
____

5. ______________________________
____

6. ______________________________
____
____

7. ______________________________
____

ENTREPRENEUR Greig Clark/College Pro Painters

ANSWERS TO DISCUSSION QUESTIONS (text, p. 462)

1. ______________________________

2. ______________________________

3. ______________________________
____

4. ______________________________

5. ______________________________

6. ______________________________

 Name________________ Date________________

Summary Exercise (text, p. 464)

Cash Receipts Journal

CASH RECEIPTS JOURNAL — Page 37

DATE	PARTICULARS	OTHER ACCOUNTS CR			ACCOUNTS RECEIVABLE CR	SALES TAX PAYABLE CR	SALES CR	REF. NO.	BANK DR
		ACCOUNT	P.R.	AMOUNT					

Travel Trailers

Name ______________________ Date ______________________

Cash Payments Journal

DATE	PARTICULARS	OTHER ACCOUNTS DR			WAGES DR	DRAWINGS DR	ACCOUNTS PAYABLE DR	REF. NO.	BANK CR
		ACCOUNT	P.R.	AMOUNT					

 Name__________ Date__________

Cash Payments Journal (cont.)

Travel Trailers

Name ____________________ Date ____________________

Purchases Journal

PURCHASES JOURNAL

Page 74

DATE		PARTICULARS	OTHER ACCOUNTS DR			FREIGHT-IN DR	SUPPLIES DR	PURCHASES DR	REF. NO.	ACCOUNTS PAYABLE CR
			ACCOUNT	P.R.	AMOUNT					

Travel Trailers

Name________________________ Date________________

Sales Journal

SALES JOURNAL

Page 19

DATE		PARTICULARS	REF. NO.			SALES TAX PAYABLE CR	SALES CR	ACCOUNTS RECEIVABLE DR

Travel Trailers

Name________________________ Date________________

General Journal

GENERAL JOURNAL PAGE 5

DATE 19 —		PARTICULARS	P.R.	DEBIT	CREDIT

Travel Trailers

Name____________________ Date________________

General Journal (cont.)

GENERAL JOURNAL

PAGE 6

DATE		PARTICULARS	P.R.	DEBIT	CREDIT

General Ledger

GENERAL LEDGER

ACCOUNT Bank NO. 101

DATE 19—		PARTICULARS	P.R.	DEBIT	CREDIT	D/C	BALANCE
May	31	Forwarded	–			D	11 751.75

ACCOUNT Accounts Receivable NO. 110

DATE 19—		PARTICULARS	P.R.	DEBIT	CREDIT	D/C	BALANCE
May	31	Forwarded	—			D	2 483.25

ACCOUNT Merchandise Inventory NO. 115

DATE 19—		PARTICULARS	P.R.	DEBIT	CREDIT	D/C	BALANCE
May	31	Forwarded	—			D	125 423.–

General Ledger (cont.)

ACCOUNT Supplies **NO.** 120

DATE 19—		PARTICULARS	P.R.	DEBIT	CREDIT	D/C	BALANCE
May	31	Forwarded	–			D	1 151 –

ACCOUNT Prepaid Insurance **NO.** 125

DATE 19—		PARTICULARS	P.R.	DEBIT	CREDIT	D/C	BALANCE
May	31	Forwarded	—			D	2 650 –

ACCOUNT Equipment **NO.** 130

DATE 19—		PARTICULARS	P.R.	DEBIT	CREDIT	D/C	BALANCE
May	31	Forwarded	—			D	28 472 –

ACCOUNT Delivery Truck **NO.** 140

DATE 19—		PARTICULARS	P.R.	DEBIT	CREDIT	D/C	BALANCE
May	31	Forwarded	–			D	22 000 –

Travel Trailers

Name ______________________ Date ______________

General Ledger (cont.)

ACCOUNT Accounts Payable **NO.** 201

DATE 19—		PARTICULARS	P.R.	DEBIT	CREDIT	D/C	BALANCE
May	31	Forwarded	—			C	19 987 –

ACCOUNT Bank Loan **NO.** 205

DATE 19—		PARTICULARS	P.R.	DEBIT	CREDIT	D/C	BALANCE
May	31	Forwarded				C	120 000 –

ACCOUNT Sales Tax Payable **NO.** 210

DATE 19—		PARTICULARS	P.R.	DEBIT	CREDIT	D/C	BALANCE
May	31	Forwarded				C	1 694 24

ACCOUNT C. Fowler, Capital **NO.** 305

DATE 19—		PARTICULARS	P.R.	DEBIT	CREDIT	D/C	BALANCE
May	31	Forwarded	—			C	43 410 51

Travel Trailers

Name ______________________ Date ______________

General Ledger (cont.)

ACCOUNT C. Fowler, Drawings **NO.** 310

DATE 19 —		PARTICULARS	P.R.	DEBIT	CREDIT	D/C	BALANCE
May	31	Forwarded	—			D	15 000 –

ACCOUNT Sales **NO.** 405

DATE 19 —		PARTICULARS	P.R.	DEBIT	CREDIT	D/C	BALANCE
May	31	Forwarded	—			C	189 423 51

ACCOUNT Discounts Earned **NO.** 410

DATE 19 —		PARTICULARS	P.R.	DEBIT	CREDIT	D/C	BALANCE
May	31	Forwarded	—			C	1 034 20

General Ledger (cont.)

ACCOUNT Purchases NO. 505

DATE 19—		PARTICULARS	P.R.	DEBIT	CREDIT	D/C	BALANCE
May	31		—			D	96 5 8 1 75

ACCOUNT Freight-in NO. 510

DATE 19—		PARTICULARS	P.R.	DEBIT	CREDIT	D/C	BALANCE
May	31	Forwarded	—			D	1 1 7 4 72

ACCOUNT Bank Charges and Interest NO. 515

DATE 19—		PARTICULARS	P.R.	DEBIT	CREDIT	D/C	BALANCE
May	31	Forwarded	—			D	4 5 1 6 50

ACCOUNT Delivery Expense NO. 520

DATE 19—		PARTICULARS	P.R.	DEBIT	CREDIT	D/C	BALANCE
May	31	Forwarded	—			D	5 6 5 0 20

Travel Trailers

Name________________ Date________________

General Ledger (cont.)

ACCOUNT Insurance Expense **NO.** 525

DATE 19—		PARTICULARS	P.R.	DEBIT	CREDIT	D/C	BALANCE

ACCOUNT Light and Heat **NO.** 530

DATE 19—		PARTICULARS	P.R.	DEBIT	CREDIT	D/C	BALANCE
May	31	Forwarded	—			D	4 3 5 0 40

ACCOUNT Miscellaneous Expense **NO.** 535

DATE 19—		PARTICULARS	P.R.	DEBIT	CREDIT	D/C	BALANCE
May	31	Forwarded	—			D	9 9 4 58

Travel Trailers

Name ______________________ Date ________________

General Ledger (cont.)

ACCOUNT Rent **NO.** 540

DATE 19 —		PARTICULARS	P.R.	DEBIT	CREDIT	D/C	BALANCE
May	31	Forwarded	—			D	6 2 5 0 –

ACCOUNT Supplies Expense **NO.** 545

DATE 19 —		PARTICULARS	P.R.	DEBIT	CREDIT	D/C	BALANCE

ACCOUNT Telephone **NO.** 550

DATE 19 —		PARTICULARS	P.R.	DEBIT	CREDIT	D/C	BALANCE
May	31	Forwarded	—			D	1 3 7 6 20

ACCOUNT Wages **NO.** 555

DATE 19 —		PARTICULARS	P.R.	DEBIT	CREDIT	D/C	BALANCE
May	31	Forwarded	—			D	45 7 2 4 11

 Name ______________ Date ______________

General Ledger (cont.)

ACCOUNT Income Summary NO. 600

DATE 19—		PARTICULARS	P.R.	DEBIT	CREDIT	D/C	BALANCE

ACCOUNTS RECEIVABLE LEDGER

ACCOUNT B. Fraser 15 Gray Street NO.

DATE 19—		PARTICULARS	P.R.	DEBIT	CREDIT	D/C	BALANCE
May	31	Forwarded # 634	—			D	367.50

ACCOUNT W. Hoyle 49 First Street NO.

DATE 19—		PARTICULARS	P.R.	DEBIT	CREDIT	D/C	BALANCE
May	31	Forwarded # 635	—			D	78.75

Travel Trailers

Name ______________________ Date ______________

Accounts Receivable Ledger (cont.)

ACCOUNT A. Newman 250 Fort Road NO.

DATE 19—		PARTICULARS	P.R.	DEBIT	CREDIT	D/C	BALANCE
May	31	Forwarded # 629	—			D	262 50

ACCOUNT Schell Brothers 96 Garrison Avenue NO.

DATE 19—		PARTICULARS	P.R.	DEBIT	CREDIT	D/C	BALANCE
May	31	Forwarded # 633				D	1060 50

ACCOUNT N. Thompson 20 Wilson Avenue NO.

DATE 19—		PARTICULARS	P.R.	DEBIT	CREDIT	D/C	BALANCE
May	31	Forwarded # 630	—			D	624 75

Travel Trailers

Name______________________ Date______________

Accounts Receivable Ledger (cont.)

ACCOUNT L. Walker 4 Dennis Avenue NO.

DATE 19—		PARTICULARS	P.R.	DEBIT	CREDIT	D/C	BALANCE
May	31	Forwarded # 631	—			D	89.25

ACCOUNTS PAYABLE LEDGER

ACCOUNT Double-G Industries Manortown NO.

DATE 19—		PARTICULARS	P.R.	DEBIT	CREDIT	D/C	BALANCE
May	31	Forwarded # 420	—			C	10 575 –

ACCOUNT Maynard's Cartage 49 Larry Lane NO.

DATE 19—		PARTICULARS	P.R.	DEBIT	CREDIT	D/C	BALANCE

Travel Trailers

Name ______________________ Date ____________________

Accounts Payable Ledger (cont.)

ACCOUNT Modern Mobile Homes West City NO.

DATE 19—		PARTICULARS	P.R.	DEBIT	CREDIT	D/C	BALANCE
May	31	Forwarded # 2213	—			C	2100 –

ACCOUNT National Hardware 64 Venture Street NO.

DATE 19—		PARTICULARS	P.R.	DEBIT	CREDIT	D/C	BALANCE
May	31	Forwarded # 2309	—			C	2787 –

ACCOUNT Parker Manufacturing 10 Bergen Street NO.

DATE 19—		PARTICULARS	P.R.	DEBIT	CREDIT	D/C	BALANCE

ACCOUNT Windsor Manufacturing Windsor NO.

DATE 19—		PARTICULARS	P.R.	DEBIT	CREDIT	D/C	BALANCE
May	31	Forwarded # 404	—			C	4525 –

Travel Trailers

Name____________________ Date____________________

General Ledger Trial Balance

Travel Trailers

Name________________________ Date________________

Subsidiary Ledger Trial Balances

____

____

____

ACCOUNTS RECEIVABLE LEDGER, JUNE 30, 19 —		
ACCOUNTS PAYABLE LEDGER, JUNE 30, 19 —		

Travel Trailers

Name__________________________ Date____________________

Work Sheet

ACCOUNTS	TRIAL BALANCE		ADJUSTMENTS		INCOME STATEMENT		BALANCE SHEET	
	DR	CR	DR	CR	DR	CR	DR	CR

Work Sheet (cont.)

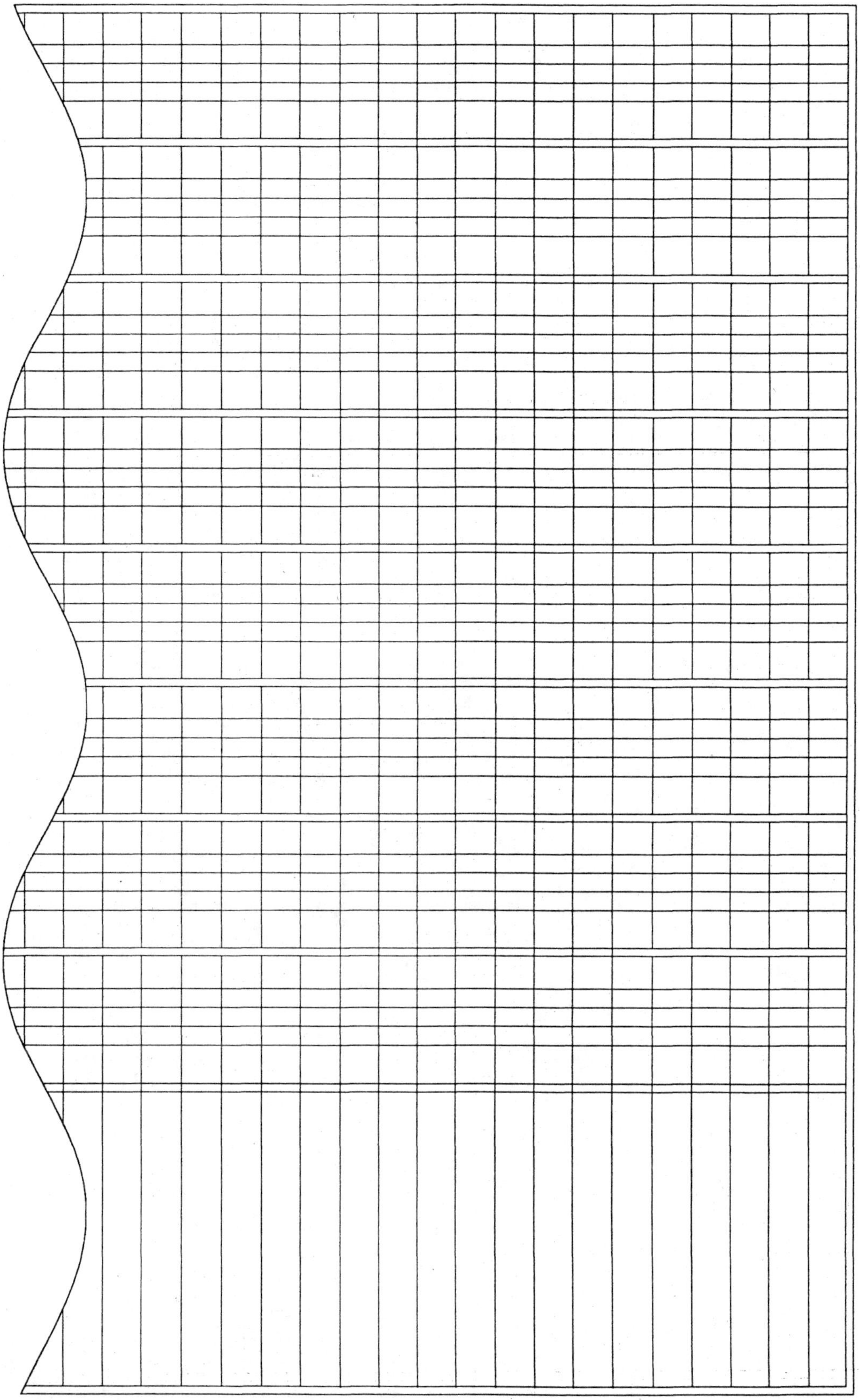

Travel Trailers

Name____________________ Date________________

Balance Sheet

Travel Trailers

Name____________________ Date_______________

Income Statement

Travel Trailers

Name ______________________ Date ______________

Post-Closing Trial Balance